FRIENDSHIP AND LOVE, ETHICS AND POLITICS

The Natalie Zemon Davis Annual Lecture Series
at Central European University, Budapest

FRIENDSHIP AND LOVE, ETHICS AND POLITICS

Studies in Mediaeval and Early Modern History

Eva Österberg

Central European University Press

Budapest – New York

© 2010 by Eva Österberg

Published in 2010 by

Central European University Press
An imprint of the
Central European University Share Company
Nádor utca 11, H-1051 Budapest, Hungary
Tel: +36-1-327-3138 or 327-3000
Fax: +36-1-327-3183
E-mail: ceupress@ceu.hu
Website: www.ceupress.com

400 West 59th Street, New York NY 10019, USA
Tel: +1-212-547-6932
Fax: +1-646-557-2416
E-mail: mgreenwald@sorosny.org

Cover design and layout by Péter Tóth

ISBN 978 963 9776 60 9
ISSN 1996 1197

Library of Congress Cataloging-in-Publication Data
Österberg, Eva, 1942-
Friendship and love, ethics and politics: studies in mediaeval and early `
modern history / Eva Österberg. p. cm.
(The Natalie Zemon Davis annual lecture series at Central European
University, Budapest)
Includes bibliographical references and index.
ISBN 978-9639776609
1. Friendship--Europe--History. 2. Love--Europe--History.
3. Sex--Europe--History. I. Title. II. Series.

BF575.F66O76 2010 177'.62--dc22 2009036364

Printed in Hungary by Akadémia Nyomda, Martonvásár

Contents

Preface

The Natalie Zemon Davis annual lecture series at the Central European University has given me the opportunity to reformulate in English some of the interpretations of friendship, love, and sexuality in premodern Europe that I have put forward in my Swedish work.[1] These are themes with important ethical and existential implications, as well as a political and cultural subtext. The lively discussions following my lectures in Budapest in November 2008 inspired me to develop my ideas, and I am truly grateful to Natalie, several colleagues, and the graduate students at the CEU for their constructive and rewarding remarks on these occasions. I hope this book will reflect just how much I profited from our enjoyable discussions in Budapest.

I was deeply honored to be invited to the CEU to give the Natalie Zemon Davis annual lecture series.

1

Natalie and I met for the first time when she was touring Sweden following the publication in Swedish of her book on Martin Guerre. Since then I have had the privilege of working with her on the Comité International des Sciences Historique (CISH), organizing the world congresses of history in Oslo 2000 and Sydney 2005. On several occasions she has been a much admired and appreciated guest at the department of history here at Lund University, where she has given lectures and generously contributed to the research of our graduate students from the National Doctoral School in History by commenting on their papers. No wonder it evoked such general enthusiasm not only amongst my fellow historians but across the university as whole when she was awarded an honorary degree in the mediaeval cathedral in Lund. In her inimitably sensitive, wise, and charming way, Natalie has been like a mentor to me. She is an enduring example to all historians, dazzling in her capacity to seek out, analyze, and communicate the multi-faceted expressions of human life, with all its variations in religion, gender, geography, language, or social and political context. As Lynn Hunt so neatly put it, Natalie has "brought a unique blend of charisma, enthusiasm and good sense to the study and teaching of history." She has also demonstrated again and again that it is possible to combine profound, innovative interpretation and a thorough critical examination of the sources with artistic brilliance in the writing of history. Truly a remarkable example!

In Budapest, Gábor Klaniczay, his staff, colleagues, and graduate students in the Mediaeval Studies Department and the History Department helped to make my visit both pleasant and inspiring. I am most grateful for their warm welcome, liberal hospitality, and animated conversation. I was also fortunate to be invited to join several excursions in Budapest, arranged by Gábor and his colleagues at Collegium Budapest, as a part of an engrossing conference on the remaking of the urban landscape. Thank you all old and new friends, from the bottom of my heart!

I am also grateful to Alan Crozier and Charlotte Merton who, in different ways, have helped me to make my manuscript comprehensible. Charlotte checked the final manuscript with both skill and enthusiasm.

Eva Österberg

Note

[1] See, for example, Eva Österberg, ed., *Jämmerdal och fröjdesal. Kvinnor i stormaktstidens Sverige*, Stockholm, 1997; Eva Österberg, *Vänskap— en lång historia*, Stockholm, 2007.

Chapter 1

Friendship, Love, and Sexuality in Premodern Times

Themes and problems

Personal life problematized

As Michel Foucault said, we academics ought always to ask ourselves why something suddenly becomes a scholarly issue. Why do we begin to mull over something that until then had appeared natural and self-evident? Why when faced with a given situation does it suddenly seem appropriate to find new words and categories to reflect more deeply on a phenomenon we previously only ever noticed in passing? "Why does this happen?" asks Foucault. What intellectual, political, or social forces impel such a problematization?[1]

This was more than relevant when historians began to reflect on friendship, love, and sexuality as serious scholarly themes some decades ago. Friendship, love, and sex are indeed enduring topics of conversation in everyday life, be it in the tearoom at work, at parties, or in the popular culture of the West. Yet most people today would not see their friends or lovers as anything other than a personal, private matter. The majority of Europeans believe that having friends or finding an outlet for their sexuality is something natural and uncontroversial, and hardly a matter for state, judicial, or political interference.

Naturally there are exceptions, above all the forms of sexuality that are still forbidden by law and that arouse most people's disgust, for example rape, adults' sexual relations with children, and the trafficking of young, poor women to better-off regions in the world to be exploited as prostitutes. Nor does friendship wholly escape society's control. Regulations on conflict-of-interest and disqualifications from nomination to public office are intended to avoid accusations that people have overstepped the mark of what is understood as legitimate in a Western democracy, in order to hand out favors to their friends. Nor does the State hold it legitimate for organized crime to command loyalty, despite as in the Mafia's case trying to sugar the pill with the rhetoric of friendship and family life.

Aside from such illegitimate relationships, friendship and love–sexuality belong primarily to a sphere where trust and privacy are meant to reign. In any event, this is how it is expressed in social scientists' models. Anthony Giddens has argued that modern people have an "environment of trust" to which elective close relationships held together by sexuality or friendship are central, matched by trust in abstractions such as the State. By contrast, premodern trust was placed largely in kinship, the local community, or God.[2]

Love, sexuality, and friendship are thus viewed in the modern age as things that belong to our private lives. It was therefore logical that historical research in the twentieth century long ignored love, sexuality, and friendship. When the historian's craft became a professionalized discipline towards the end of the nineteenth century and beginning of the twentieth, with the advent of a methodology, special journals, and university departments, the field of study was primarily defined as the official life of the nation state. Politics, state finances, wars and peace treaties, the great men who had led the development of various European countries down the centuries—these were the themes that historians cherished in the first part of the twentieth century.

Not until much later did the historians' scope widen in any significant way. Finally social history burst on the scene in the 1960s with a direct challenge to the discipline of history, introducing the idea of history from below, with its investigation of the living conditions and turbulent existence of farmhands, laborers, and the poor. Social history also included demography; accordingly, the results of love and sexuality, marriage and birth, were counted and analyzed. Not even then, though, were the complex cultural phenomena of love, sexuality, and friendship rated as a field of historical study.

It took another couple of decades, and at least two more historiographical turns (anthropological and linguistic), before sexuality and love entered historical debate with any seriousness. Michel Foucault's books on the history of sexuality were unmistakably pioneering works of a challenging kind.[3] They have been followed up by cultural historians as well as gender historians, who have pursued the fundamental issues of the different ideological and political means by which heterosexuality is construed as a social norm, whilst other forms of love and sexuality have been denied, forbidden, or controlled.[4]

It has taken even longer for historians to recognize the importance of the issues implicit in the different definitions and functions of friendship over the centuries, not to mention the various roles friends have played in society, and the combination of ethical–existential and social–political dimensions involved in the exercise of friendship.[5]

Indeed, historical books and articles that take friendship as their main theme are still rare.[6] Yet very recently an increasing interest in friendship can be detected, both in everyday life and in scholarly work. To name only a few scholars, the philosopher Jacques Derrida, the sociologist Ray Pahl, and the Norwegian philosopher Helge Snare have all published on friendship, and several anthropologists have dealt with both friendship and sexuality. Long historical perspectives are still uncommon, however, although experts on the Middle Ages have written about friendship as part of the wider social context of group dependency.[7]

Thus until very recently, friendship, love, and sexuality have been almost nonexistent in modern historical research, and wholly absent from textbooks and conferences. It is only lately, for example, that friendship became the theme for a session at a world congress of history; this happened in Sydney 2005, where I was the commentator for an inspiring panel debate organized by the British-Israeli historian Naomi Tadmor.

Why, we might well ask ourselves, do we find ourselves caught up in this new discussion of close relationships now, at the start of the twenty-first century? Why now conferences on social networks—networks now seen as essential components of modern society—despite the fact that twentieth-century democracies were to such a degree formal meritocracies, constructed around institutions and regulated bureaucratic routines? Ray Pahl has argued that personal networks and personal solidarity seem to be becoming more usual than "geographical or work-based" communities. "The social zeitgeist of the early twenty-first century is democratic, anti-authoritarian and egalitarian," he continues. The upshot is that we give priority to close relationships with friends whom we have chosen ourselves.[8]

There is certainly something to Pahl's suggestion. For myself, I believe the renewed interest not least in friendship is linked to an increasing distrust of modernity and twentieth-century organizations that to a certain extent characterizes the present discourse, whether we call it late modern or postmodern.[9] Zygmunt Bauman's carefully drawn distinctions pinpoint this brilliantly. He readily admits that we in the West live in modern societies largely distinguished by a strong State, democratic institutions, and established interest groups. Yet we have perhaps become somewhat more reserved towards modernity as a hegemonic mode of thought, and we no longer trust as much in the state's ability to solve individuals' problems. Instead, people today are more open to informal, personal solutions and flexible networks.[10] At the same time, for example, women's history in recent years has been able to show just how important friendship was in the high modern era for those who found themselves excluded from formal political institutions. Friendships and personal networks were decisive for women when, at the start of the twentieth century, they began their struggle for universal suffrage, peace, and social justice.[11]

There are several reasons why historical research today gives greater weight to close, informal relationships. At heart it stems from our finding a reason to problematize modernity, the dividing line between private and public, and the individual's ability to handle his or her situation alone. There is also more than a grain of truth in the idea that historians have become more curious about groups that were previously invisible, and who for so long remained hidden from view when the great men of public life dominated historiography.

Friendship and love in the mediaeval and early modern period

In a longer perspective, the twentieth-century custom of not giving priority to friendship in serious scholarly debate is far from self-evident. In classical and mediaeval society, for example, intellectual discourse revolved around friendship, as was the case with Aristotle, Cicero, Seneca, or Bernard of Clairvaux. In reality, friendships, much like sexuality and love, served to mould the social and political alliances that were quite simply essential to the fabric of society. As yet there were no effective public institutions to meet the populace's need for security and protection. As I will attempt to demonstrate, since close relationships were not only thought to be a matter of pleasant social gatherings and intimate relationships in privacy, but just as much a matter of *ethics and politics*, they also invited the attention of the State and the Church.

To be a historian, to write about intimate relationships and friendship over the centuries, is thus in my view not only—or primarily—a matter of narrating fascinating micro-stories of closely involved individuals and their cultural backgrounds, even though I may do that too. Rather it is a matter of analyzing the *long-term, principal changes* in the intellectual and political discourses on love and friendship to reveal the ethical and political implications of such relationships, the purposes they served in different periods, and their impact not only on other social discourses but also on social change.

My prime concerns thus are the patterns of change over time: the ways that public officials, philosophers, politicians, the Church, and monastic authorities, but also other people like merchants or clergymen, have thought and talked about friendship, love, and sexuality. It is here, in everyday exchanges, that the full implications of close relationship practices are revealed, whether implicitly or explicitly.

However, it is impossible in a few extended lectures (or for that matter in a monograph) to do justice to the full cultural spectrum of such practices. It must suffice to note that from classical antiquity to the present such forms as friendship and intimate relationships have taken *in reality* vary not only according to gender and age, but also to social position, ethnicity, and personality. I will only allude to some of these variations here, and will instead concentrate on the *discourses on friendship and sexuality–love and their changes over time.* These discourses may be found stated explicitly by philosophers or representatives of the Church or State, but equally they can be discovered embedded in autobiographies, letters, literary fiction, sermons, or in court records.

My approach means that I draw examples from different kinds of material produced within Europe. As I am an expert on Scandinavian history, it is only natural that I set out to incorporate a few detailed analyses of sources from the Nordic countries as well. For those able to read Scandinavian languages, I refer you to my book in Swedish for more examples and case studies than can be included here.[12] In the book, published in 2007, I take stock of my research, focusing on friendship over an extremely long time span, from classical antiquity to modernity. Both in my lectures in Budapest and in this book, on the other hand, I specifically address *friendship in the mediaeval and early modern period against the background of classical thought.* I also pause in the final chapter to consider *love and sexuality in the early modern period.* Friendship and love are linked for a number of reasons. Both friendship and love were integral to the wide definitions (*philia*, *amicitia*) of close relationships used by the classical philosophers, definitions that have been crucial to European thought on the nature of such relationships and their function ever since.

Subsequently the boundary between love and friendship has become sharper, however. To some extent this came about because both friendship and love–sexuality have at times taken on forms that mediaeval and early modern authorities—both secular and spiritual—viewed as inappropriate or downright dangerous, and therefore attempted to regulate or ban. Thus the principal questions addressed in the coming chapters are:

What form did the *discourse* take amongst philosophers, clerical and monastic thinkers, jurists, and state officials when it came to friendship and love, when classical ideas were transmitted to the mediaeval and early modern period? Which variations were recognized in the form such relationships took, and what functions were they said to have?

On the basis of correspondence, diaries, or autobiographies, for example, what can we say about how friendships were *shaped in practice*, and what did people outside the ruling elite think about close relationships?

To what degree did friendship in these older periods transcend the distinctions between *private and public* that then existed?

Having friends and lovers is by its nature a social activity; we reach out to other people in human interaction. But together with others we also learn to know ourselves, a truth recognized long ago by the classical philosophers. One strand of historical research identifies an increased individualism in Europe that evolved over an extended period of history, in which particular eras such as the Renaissance and the Enlightenment meant a step forwards for the autonomy of the individual, self-awareness, and self-reflection. There is thus good cause to wonder whether any such changes in *subject-formation*, or the degree of individualism, can be linked to notions of friendship in the genre that has long been held to personify subject-formation like no other, *autobiography*.

In the early modern period, when state-formation characterized European political development, when, why, and to what degree did institutions of power or individual thinkers consider it a priority to *caution against friendship or love–sexuality*? Which forms of close relationship did the State or Church have reason to view as a *threat*, and by the same token which did they attempt to safeguard? What form did the restrictions placed on people by law and legal custom take?

I would be the first to admit that these are broad questions. It goes without saying that I cannot hope to address all the issues thrown out by this line of questioning in the space of the three lectures that led to this little book. My hope is that the questions themselves, taken with the examples and partial answers I offer in the following chapters, will awaken the reader's curiosity. In the best case they will lead to new research on a theme that I expect to become increasingly significant in society for ethical and existential reasons, not to mention political reasons. The cultural history of friendship and love is not yet concluded.

The structure of the book

In chapter 2 I consider how the leading classical authorities viewed the close relationships that came under the rubric of the Greek term *philia*. As I have already noted, they included relationships that we today would call love. For this reason, therefore, it behoves us to consider friendship and love–sexuality in parallel; in the philosophy that the West has adopted as the fount of all discourses on friendship and love, both phenomena are contained within the same term. Friendship is the focus of chapters 2 and

3, while chapter 4 is given over to a discussion of the discourse on good and deviant sexuality–love in the early modern period.

Modern scholars have spilled a great deal of ink in defining the exact differences between love and friendship. The Italian sociologist Francesco Alberoni points out that love normally comprises passion and sexuality. Love is also exclusive; we love only one person at a time. We can, however, have more than one friend. Love involves the strongest ties, Alberoni writes, while the ties of friendship are less intense. Friendship, he argues in another significant phrase, is the *moral form of Eros*; it connects people who are essentially equals. It also builds on respect, something that is not necessarily the case when we fall in love, for that is a sensation based on physical attraction, passion. Instead, friendship is a *chain of meetings*, a *serial solidarity* that gives pleasure. Love can be a source of suffering; it throws us into turmoil, bringing now pain, now happiness. Not so friendship. In truth, time spent with a friend ought to be pleasant; otherwise the friendship comes to an end. Friendship is fundamentally a moral relationship; ultimately a friend who fails us is no friend at all.[13]

Above all, in chapter 2, I discuss how views on friendship changed, and how friendly relationships might have functioned in mediaeval and early modern society, in terms of the distinction between private and public. My argument is built partly on what I have found in the European philosophers' and clerics' writings, and on analyses of St Birgitta's visions and the narratives of mediaeval Icelandic sagas. But I also consider legal material from Sweden, and draw significant examples from the correspondence and diaries of people from different social groups in Britain and Sweden in the seventeenth and eighteenth centuries. One interesting observation is that the state gradually found reason to legislate against what was seen as the danger of friendship, namely corruption in conjunction with the administration of justice.

Chapter 3 focuses on a handful of seminal European autobiographies from Augustine to Rousseau. This is set against the background of Aristotle's contention that man attains self-knowledge and happiness through the friendship of others, as well as the common notion of autobiography as "the genre of egocentrism." I demonstrate that the chief focus in these autobiographies is the writer's relationship with God, existential angst, intellectual development, or the wish to go down to posterity as unique. None the less, several of the autobiographers also offer interesting reflections on the nature of friendship, and all of them have something to say on the subject of friends or lovers who have been important to them.

While friendship is the principal theme of chapters 2 and 3, in chapter 4 I discuss sexuality and love, and the distinction between the acceptable forms of love–sexuality on the one hand and the forbidden forms on the other. The empirical example here is Scandinavia, and Sweden in particular, in the early modern period. The bulk of the material is drawn from legal sources, but sermons are also used. This gives me opportunity to evaluate my approach in the light both of Foucault and of European research on the Reformation as a gendered history. Invoking the terminology of gender studies, we can speak of the judicial and religious discourse in Sweden in this period as construed heteronormatively, and applied with an effectiveness that was unusual. The legislation on prohibited sexuality was tightened in much the same period as the early modern central state identified dangerous expressions of friendship. However, I argue that the consequences of the Reformation for women were ambiguous.

Finally, chapter 5 consists of a short survey in which I reflect on my conclusions in a broader perspective.

Notes

[1] See, for example, Michel Foucault, *Histoire de la sexualité I: La volonté de savoir*, Paris, 1976.

[2] See, for example, Anthony Giddens, *The Consequences of Modernity*, Cambridge, 1990; Anthony Giddens, *Modernity and Self-Identity. Self and Society in the Late Modern Age*, Cambridge, 1991.

[3] Michel Foucault, *Histoire de la sexualité* I–III, Paris, 1976.

[4] See chapter 4 for further references.

[5] For a more extensive discussion see Eva Österberg, *Vänskap—en lång historia*, Stockholm, 2007, pp. 9–48, 279–295.

[6] My own recent book on friendship is one of a few examples of a historical investigation of friendship in a long-term perspective: Eva Österberg, *Vänskap—en lång historia*. Lars Hermanson has published a book on friendship in the Middle Ages, drawing on mediaeval Scandinavian sources: Lars Hermanson, *Bärande band. Vänskap, kärlek och brödraskap i det medeltida Nordeuropa, ca 1000–1200*, Lund, 2009. An important early contribution was made by the American-Danish historian Brian McGuire, *Friendship and Community: The Monastic Experience 350–1250*, Kalamazoo, 1988. Similarly, few social scientists have made friendship their particular interest, although naturally there are exceptions, amongst them Francesco Alberoni, *L'amicizia*, Milan, 1984; Jacques Derrida, *Politics of Friendship*, London, 1997; and Ray Pahl, *On Friendship*, Malden, Mass., 2000.

[7] For example, Jacques Derrida, *Politics of Friendship*; Ray Pahl, *On Friendship*; Allan Silver, *Public and Private in Thought and Practice*, Chicago, 1998; Helge Svare, *Vennskap*, Oslo, 2004; Britta Lundgren, *Den ofullkomliga vänskapen*, Stockholm, 1995; Lars Hermanson, *Släkt, vänner och makt. En studie av elitens politiska kultur i 1100-talets Danmark*, Göte-

21

borg, 2000; Gerd Althoff, *Verwandte, Freunde und Getreue. Zum politischen Stellenweer der Gruppenbindungen im früheren Mittelalter*, Darmstadt, 1990; Gerd Althoff, "Friendship and Political Order" in Julian Haseldine, ed., *Friendship in Medieval Europe*, Stroud, Gloucs., 1999, pp. 91–105; Gerd Althoff, *Family, friends and followers: the political importance of group bonds in the early Middle Ages*, New York, 2004; L. Hermanson, T. Småberg, J. Sigurdsson, J. Danneskiold-Samsöe, eds., *Vänner, patroner och klienter. Norden 900–1800*, Report to the 26th Nordic history conference, Reykjavik 8–12 August 2007. Reykjavik, 2007.

[8] Ray Pahl, *On Friendship*, p. 2.

[9] For a more detailed discussion see Eva Österberg, *Vänskap—en lång historia*, pp. 25–29.

[10] Zygmunt Bauman, *Intimations of Post-Modernity*, New York, 1992 p. vii ff.

[11] A couple of excellent Scandinavian examples are Irene Andersson, *Kvinnor mot krig. Aktioner och nätverk för fred 1914–1940*, Lund, 2001; Sif Bokholm, *En kvinnoröst i manssamhället. Agda Montelius 1850–1920*, Stockholm, 2000; and Christina Florin, *Kvinnor får röst. Kön, känslor och politisk kultur i kvinnornas rösträttsrörelse*, Stockholm, 2006.

[12] Eva Österberg, *Vänskap—en lång historia*.

[13] See Francesco Alberoni, *Vänskap*, Gothenburg, 1987; and Francesco Alberoni, *Jag älskar dig*, Gothenburg, 1996. Both works are discussed in Eva Österberg, *Vänskap—en lång historia*, pp. 65–67.

Chapter 2

Challenging the Private–Public Dichotomy

Friendship in mediaeval and early modern society

Res privata and res publica

Acknowledgement of the historical relevance of the private–public dichotomy is often associated with Jürgen Habermas's influential theory, focusing as it does on the bourgeois public sphere in the eighteenth and nineteenth centuries. In his view, this public sphere was characterized by open communication, rational argument, and reason. He also views it as something new, in stark contrast to the representative public sphere of premodern society, in which hierarchical power presented itself to the people in what was to all intents and purposes one-way communication.[1] In recent decades, however, Habermas's ideas have been challenged, not least by historians studying popular culture, gender, or the early modern period. The British-Israeli historian Naomi Tadmor perceptively summarizes the debate as follows:

If Habermas presented the public sphere as bourgeois, modern, male, secular, rational, and structured essentially around the late seventeenth and eighteenth centuries, current scholars portray it as popular, early modern, wrought with religious debate, … crossing gender boundaries, and active since the early seventeenth century or even since post-Reformation debates.[2]

In his theory, Habermas deals primarily with the communicative, debating aspect of the public sphere, stressing the importance of men's political clubs, liberal debates in daily newspapers, political speeches, and the like. His critics have added to the variety of debates in public spheres with an understanding of the semi-political culture of the ladies' salons of eighteenth-century France, for instance. Others have contributed with examples of possible popular forms of public sphere in much earlier periods. Taking into account the relative independence of the majority of Swedes in the early modern period—the peasantry owned their land, and even had a voice in the parliament—Swedish historians have seen parish assemblies and district courts as serving as a kind of popular public sphere.[3]

The private sphere, in contrast, has been connected with family life in a narrower sense, embracing family, kin, and sometimes servants. This is true of both Habermas himself and those who have revised his thesis. Indeed, they differ little in their definition of the private sphere.

However, the private–public dichotomy per se long predates the Habermas debate. The two concepts are derived from the Latin *res privata*—that which takes place in family life—and *res publica*—that which concerns public life, the state, and official tasks and responsibilities. In that sense the divergence between private and public life, as Georges Duby rightly points out, is one of *place and power.* Private refers to those places where no one may intrude unless they are invited, where family business is handled without the interference of authorities outside the household, where life is intimate and informal. Public, meanwhile, refers to places where people meet, be it in the streets or in official buildings, to debate and decide common civil matters; that is, to execute social power. Regardless of period, therefore, a distinction is always drawn between private and public. Such distinctions are present in every society, although not necessarily in the same manner. As Duby himself notes, the exact course of the dividing line may be fluid.[4]

Furthermore, there may have been social relationships, either real or notional, that tended to blur the dichotomy, to cross the dividing line. One in particular that did much to obscure the distinction between public and private in premodern times was friendship.

The classical philosophy of friendship

The classical philosophy of friendship, represented by Aristotle, Cicero and Seneca, in fact included the possibility of a link between the private sphere and the public sphere where the business of the city-state was to be handled skillfully by good men.

The starting point for Aristotle (384–322 BC) in his *Nichomachean Ethics* is the idea that man is an active social being who looks not only to his own happiness but equally to the common weal. The relationship between friends is defined—much as it has been ever since in the European tradition—as a personal and informal relationship based on *reciprocity* and *trust*. It is also *voluntary*, since it depends on our *choice*. We are not born into friendship in the same way as we are born into family or kinship. Lastly, ideal friendship presupposes *equality*, or at the very least either the illusion of equality or a serious wish for it. Certainly, as Aristotle admits, such equality is difficult to achieve, and in reality friends are not always perfectly equal. However, "even where people are unequal, they may be friends, as they will be equalized" because "equality and similarity constitute friendship."[5] The relationship itself thus promotes at least a sense of equality. In any case, friendship cannot be likened to a power hierarchy in which one party is clearly subordinate to the other. Friends ought to trust each other and be certain of each other's concern, in an atmosphere of informality and mutual respect.

The Greek word for close relationships was *philia*, in Latin *amicitia*. These were exceptionally broad concepts. They extended to all so-called natural relationships, such as love of a mother, brother, child, and so on, and thus encompassed both what we today would call love and what we refer to as friendship. The classical philosophers imagined that friendship could arise for several reasons, and to different ends. People become friends because of the mutual *use* they have of each other, but also because they want to find *pleasure* in the relationship—they simply want to enjoy meeting and conversing with an affable person. There is no doubt, however, that what was most important to the classical philosophers was *ideal friend-*

27

ship, that excellent, perfect friendship that could only be achieved—in the best of cases—by a very few outstandingly virtuous men, and then only if they exerted themselves. This kind of friendship would be permanent:

> It would seem that friendship or love is the natural instinct of a parent towards a child, and of a child towards a parent, ... The kinds of friendships therefore will be three, ... those whose mutual love is based upon utility do not love each other for their own sakes, but only in so far as they derive some benefit from one another. It is the same with those whose love is based upon pleasure. ... The perfect friendship or love is the friendship or love of people who are good and alike in virtue; for these people are alike in wishing each other's good, in so far as they are good, and they are good in themselves. ... Such a friendship is naturally permanent, as it unites in itself all the proper conditions of friendship. ... Friendships of this kind are likely to be rare; for such people are few. They require time and familiarity too.[6]

In my view Aristotle thought that the extraordinary kind of friendship, once it was found, was a privilege that should not be kept exclusively private.

Rather, the qualities that excellent men possessed through ideal friendship should be transferred to the social and political life of the community. Official life should profit from the friends' attainment of virtue and excellence of character, together with their capacity to form sound judgements for the benefit of the common good. They have the quality of practical wisdom, *phronesis*, which belongs to both the private and the public sphere.[7]

As a consequence, several much later scholars such as the Danish philosopher Søren Kierkegaard in the nineteenth century and Paul Ricoeur in the twentieth, have rightly argued that friendship for Aristotle was neither primarily a matter of psychology nor of sentiment. Rather, it was a matter of *ethics*—and *politics*.[8] Affection, Aristotle claims, resembles an emotion, "but friendship resembles a moral state. ... The love of friends for one another implies moral purpose, and such moral purpose is the outcome of a moral state." He also states that "friendship or love is the bond which holds states together, and that legislators set more store by it than by justice; for concord is apparently akin to friendship, and it is concord that they especially seek to promote."[9] Obviously, Aristotle defines justice and concord as the most solid of the building blocks used in state-formation. Since in his view ideal friendship creates concord, there is no problem in including friendship in the process of governing, in public life.

Intellectual historians have noted that Aristotle did not see any real difference between love and friendship, as is evident from the longer of the quotations above. Both are inherent to his concept *philia*, and the difference is a matter of degree rather than kind. For Aristotle, love is a sort of friendship, while friendship might even be combined with eroticism. This way of thinking may seem strange to modern minds. But it is less surprising if we bear in mind that Aristotle lived in a homosocial and to some extent homoerotic milieu.[10]

Similarly, friendship for Cicero was essential if men were to live a good life, in public life as well as in private. Cicero wrote his book on friendship, *Laelius* or *De amicitia*, in the years 45–44 BC. It places a disquisition on friendship in the mouth of Gaius Laelius, a statesman born in 186 BC, and a pupil of the Stoic Diogenes. Ideal friendship, according to Cicero, can really only exist between men who concur on important spiritual and temporal issues. Such a perfect friendship brings both benefits and pleasure, but they are not its source; that, instead, is virtue (*virtus*). The friendship comprises mutual kindness (*benevolentia*), consensus (*consensio*), devotion (*caritas*), and loyalty (*fidelitas*); not for nothing did friendship take its name from love ('*Amor enim, ex quo amicitia nominata est*'). Yet Cicero is clear that such an ideal relationship is not easy to attain, particularly since in reality two friends are rarely so equal as they ought to be. Both tact and generosity are called for if a sense of equality is to exist between friends. Speaking the truth can be difficult for friends, Cicero–Laelius continues; you ought to be honest, but you must be so without harshness or reproach.[11]

There are thus two crucial differences between the classical philosophy of friendship and comparable ideas in the modern period. First, love and friendship were not kept strictly apart in classical thinking. The dividing line between them was not sharp, so that friendship could be clad in the language of love, and love in the rhetoric of friendship. This remained the case for much of history. But when bourgeois society emerged in the eighteenth and nineteenth centuries, with its new views on private life, romantic love, and affective family life, the distinctions between friends and family, love and friendship, gradually became clearer.

Second and more important, ideal friendship in

classical philosophy centered on qualities that were equally beneficial to the common good. Ideal friendship was an ideology, a relationship that stretched from private to public.[12] As a matter of fact, this will turn out to have been just as relevant in subsequent centuries.[13]

Good and bad friends—mediaeval ambivalence

Let us look more closely at mediaeval thinking on friendship. To demonstrate my argument, I will discuss learned Christian thought from the cloisters, abbeys, and churches of Europe, matched with the beliefs of an insular society in the thirteenth century conveyed to us in the remarkable Icelandic family sagas. It is a deliberate choice on my part, made for several reasons. Christianity was fundamental to the hegemonic discourse in most parts of mediaeval Europe from at least the eleventh century. Naturally, only an educated elite was at leisure to elaborate and comment on the main religious texts, yet, as Aron Gurevich argues in his book on mediaeval popular culture, there is no doubt whatsoever that Church ideology and popular culture interacted.[14] Mediaeval man had a worldview, a mentality, which was suffused with magic and religion. It was through sermons, stories of miracles, and accounts of the lives of saints that religious ideas were spread; certain genres of mediaeval Latin literature were copied, distributed, and widely appreciated. In the process of popular reception, Christian ideas were probably moulded, misunderstood, and changed to some extent, but nonetheless they came to be absorbed into the general culture. True, not everyone could read Latin. But the meaning of the texts could be told and retold, and endlessly discussed. It would be fruitless to deny that these writings influenced people deeply, in spite of their recondite language.

The Icelandic sagas, meanwhile, are not only the most inspiring Nordic contribution to mediaeval world literature, they also represent an intriguing, subtle mix of pre-Christian and Christian thought, an interweaving of pagan and learned culture. Their authors may have lived on the periphery of Europe, but they were nevertheless educated men and well aware of the literature of the day, including literary fiction. The main plot in a saga often reflects broad literary themes: love, death, betrayal, and violence. Despite this, few scholars would deny that the Icelandic sagas could also be used as evidence of the mediaeval Scandinavian cultural codes that held good at the time when they were written down in the thirteenth century, even if they are not unproblematic and can only be used with great interpretative sensitivity.[15] Sagas can be analyzed to trace cultural patterns and perhaps even mentalities; just like popular culture today, they were a widely disseminated body of narratives that were dependent on oral as well as scholarly traditions.

What, then, happened in mediaeval society to the classical notion of the ideal friendship as something with a higher purpose, not merely a pleasant addition to private life? What happened to the possibility that friendship could belong to both the private and the public domain? How were the classical ideas changed in the process of Christianization, a process in which classical ideas were adapted to the ideas of the Bible and other Christian texts?

Undoubtedly, it was learned people in the Church and religious orders who carried the classical philosophy of friendship into the Middle Ages. From Aristotle, Cicero and the rest, they could adopt the concepts needed to debate and reflect on friendship. Terms such as *amicitia perfecta* (perfect friendship), *amicitia vera* (true friendship), *virtus* (virtue), and *summum bonum* (supreme good) lived on as key concepts in the mediaeval intellectual world. The challenge for Christian intellectuals, however, was to reconcile classical ideas of friendship with love of God and the ideals of monastic life.

Of course, they did have the Bible to fall back on. But, as the Danish-American historian Brian McGuire has pointed out, the Bible has very little to say about friendship. Certainly, there are passages in Proverbs, Ecclesiastes, and the story of David and Jonathan in the First Book of Samuel, for example. Proverbs in particular is concerned with loyalty. Yet it also sponsors an outlook on reality devoid of illusion, verging on the cynical: if you have gold, you will find friends, but if you become poor, you will not be able to count on them. In the New Testament, a few are shown as having been particularly close to Jesus, yet Christian love was ultimately supposed to apply to all fellow men and to be unconditional in its yearning for God. St Paul, for example, insisted on the virtue of collective friendship, shared by everyone in all the Christian congregations, as a kind of religious public community.

This then was the dilemma of mediaeval Christian reflection on friendship: those in religious orders were expected to love each other equally, and all of them were meant to share the same longing for God. The question remained to what extent abbots and abbesses could permit members of their religious communities to enter into individual friendships. And should friendship be allowed between individuals in religious institutions and those in the outside world, the latter representing quite another form of public sphere than the religious community?

Just how complicated friendship could become in mediaeval Christian Europe is a subject Brian McGuire has focused on. He underlines the fact that the Church Father Augustine of Hippo (354–430) spoke of true friendship (*amicitia vera*) as a relationship that sprang from God. Bede (672–735) coined the term *amicitia spiritualis*, spiritual friendship between the religious. Both thus tried to reformulate friendship as a spiritual relationship. Then again, friendship without qualification for Bede implied a temporal political alliance, and that was not good. In the period 850–1050 asceticism was the governing ideal in the Christian world, as McGuire points out. Friendship as a separate relationship between two individuals in a religious community was quite simply not acceptable.[16]

The period 1050–1120, on the other hand, was a period of renewal when many Christian authorities set about coining a language of friendship, and the period 1120–1180 was to be a golden age of friendship in the Christian West. The Cistercians were early in expressing an enthusiasm for friendship. Bernard of Clairvaux (1090–1153) devised a doctrine of a spiritual friendship in the shape of a five-step programme: the choice of a friend; putting the friendship to the test; the confirmation of friendship; total confidence and mutual trust; and sublimation with the friend with God in Paradise—the Christian *summum bonum*.

But above all we should note the meaning of friendship to Aelred of Rievaulx. Aelred was aware of the classical discourse on friendship, not least Cicero's. But he drew particularly on the Bible and other Christian sources as well as his own feelings and experiences. He believed there could be friendships within monastery walls that could pave the way to God. Yet at the same time he recognized the sense of frustration and envy that might arise in those who were not included whenever a pair of friends withdrew to converse privately. What is important about Aelred's writings, McGuire observes, is that he attempts to define the "correct" friendship between Christians as a spiritual, non-sexual relationship. Friends must impose restrictions upon themselves in their expression of affection.[17]

It was this problem of how to set limits on how

people in religious orders could behave that would increasingly be addressed in the Orders' regulations. In the Cistercians' statutes of the 1180s and 1190s it is deemed inappropriate for brothers to embrace one another in anything other than exceptional circumstances. Towards the end of the Middle Ages, the Franciscans were instructed that they should relate to one another as members of a family, not as particular friends. Sporadic warnings were issued by the Church against such close friendships as could lead to the risk of sexual intimacy. But generally speaking, individual friendship was to be avoided because it was thought to undermine the general solidarity of the religious community or diminish the eagerness of the collective endeavor to love God. Given these inherent complications, throughout the Middle Ages there were always religious authorities that perceived friendship as a risky undertaking. The ideal was that all the residents in a monastery would be loyal to each other and concentrate on their mutual search for God.[18]

This is the critical line of thought taken by the most famous Swedish saint, St Birgitta (1303–1373). She pictures friendship as a relationship riddled with ambiguities for the religious, a view created by her dualistic vision of the world in which the forces of good and evil clash incessantly. Thus she also writes of temporal friendship as evil and disastrous. One must enter a spiritual friendship with God, she urges, and leave behind cold and empty friendship that is but a vain conceit and contrivance. Friends who try to seduce you with worldly glory are like dirt or the hissing of a serpent. If you fall prey to them, you may find yourself trapped in the terrible moats of temptation that surround the castle of God. They represent

> ... the beauty of the world and the company and delight of worldly friends. There are many people who are content to take their ease in these moats and never care about whether they will see God in heaven. The moats are wide and deep; wide because the will of such people is far from God; deep because they confine many people to the depths of hell.[19]

Set against this, Birgitta describes the relationship between God and his faithful children as something amounting to companionable. The 'right' friends in Birgitta's view were thus those with whom you shared a devotion to God. In her dualistic world, good friends who are faithful to God can exist, but equally so can the worldly friends of whom she was deeply suspicious. However, she was prepared to admit that the religious also had an occasional need to talk with friends without discussing spiritual matters. In one of her revelations she mentions the activities that are permissible for a bishop. She includes in that category spending time with friends—in moderation. Even men of God need a little relaxation, she acknowledges. Yet God permits the company of friends not because he sets store by it, but because he realises that man is weak:

> When the meal is over and grace has been said, the bishop should make such announcements as are fitting, or conduct whatever business his episcopal office requires, or sleep a while if that would be healthful, or study books from which he can draw spiritual sustenance. After the evening meal he can enjoy the presence of his friends in a proper manner, and comfort himself with their company, for if the bow is drawn too tight, it breaks the sooner. Thus may modest enjoyment to allay the weakness of the flesh be pleasing to God.[20]

An ideal spiritual friendship that unites two good people in the search for God thus came to be accepted by most religious authorities in the Middle

Ages, although some considered the privacy of two friends problematic when seen in the light of a religious community as a whole. Private friendship should not negate solidarity with the whole religious community; rather it should interact with the community in the effort to please God. Outside, in the wider world, another community existed with which any friendly contact might result in evil temptation.

Thus different aspects of public and private are intertwined in a complex way when we discuss mediaeval religious discourses. Just as the classical philosophy of friendship held that perfect friendship had ethical and political implications that blurred the dividing line between private and public life, the Christian version of ideal friendship also aimed at something that transcended family life. Christianity, however, did not strive for a temporal political life, but a spiritual community life—and God.

Necessary alliances

What, then, of the Icelandic sagas? On one level, the sagas are often about conflict—that much is obvious. Yet it is equally clear that they are just as much about conflict that fails to materialize, about conflict averted. As Jesse Byock, Carol Clover and others have noted, the narratives in fact deal extensively with attempts to avoid conflict. They tell us of negotiations and legal solutions agreed in the *ting* or national law court, a body that was also the arena for political argument, alliance formation, and prestigious demonstrations of honor. Ian William Miller argues that the quest for honor and balance between men is the key to understanding the mentality of the sagas.[21]

The crucial fact here is that Iceland in the thirteenth and fourteenth centuries lacked a state and a king of its own. What held the country together—the forces of integration—were the law, the *ting*, and personal alliances.

Until recently, scholars have tended to emphasize kinship by blood and by marriage as the main social bond in Iceland,[22] just as in other so-called primitive societies. Marriage could secure alliances, as is apparent from both sagas and laws. As Audur Magnúsdóttir has shown, in the twelfth and thirteenth centuries concubinage was often the basis for political alliances and social loyalties, until the Church gradually succeeded in making polygamous relationships unacceptable. Compared with alliances between equal families, the association between a mistress of lower standing and a man's powerful relatives could in fact bring certain advantages to the man. The woman's family was the more dependent on the man, and was therefore inclined to show greater loyalty to the alliance. If a highborn man had several mistresses, each of whom had loyal family, he could thus call on an extensive network of allies when the need arose.[23]

However, this focus on kinship has recently come in for criticism. The anthropologist Gísli Pálsson, for example, notes that it is part of the anthropologists' tradition to prioritize kinship when they want to explain social mechanisms in primitive societies. They have tended to see kinship systems everywhere, while they have been more or less blind to informal relationships such as friendship. This is also true of analyses of the Icelandic sagas. The importance of kinship has been overemphasized because the sagas open with a rehearsal of the relevant genealogy of the leading characters in the plot. In a short study in collaboration with E.P. Durrenberger, Pálsson focuses instead on voluntary relationships within the social ambit of the sagas, and draws the conclusion that friendship alliances were immensely important. On many occasions they were struck between the wealthiest farmers and less prominent men, or between older, wiser lawmen and young hotheads. Terms of friendship were thus applied to non-equal relationships. But of course, evenly matched men could also be friends.

In fact, as Pálsson indicates, in the world of the sagas there were two kinds of social relationship that were crucial to the fabric of society: patron–client relationships, and alliances entered into voluntarily by men of equal standing. Both were founded on friendship rather than kinship. There are parallels to be found in other periods and cultures that lacked a strong state and were instead governed by great men. In such cultures, informal friendship tends to become an important social and political institution.[24]

In this context, Jón Vidar Sigurdsson and I have studied examples of friendship narrated in the mediaeval Icelandic sagas. We have shown the importance of alliances based on friendship, mutual loyalty, and gift exchange. Friendship is often more vital than kinship in societies with a bilateral kinship system, in which kin on both the father's and the mother's side are counted. This was the case in the Nordic countries, then as now. In such systems, the circle of potential kindred could be cast extremely wide: uncles, aunts, cousins and second cousins on both sides of the family. In fact it was impossible to know everyone closely, and it is not at all evident how far a sense of true loyalty to relatives extended.[25] Many relatives were quite literally distant; others were emotionally distant even if they were physically close. Thus kinship alone could not amount to life insurance; it could easily be little more than a vague, even remote, link between people that could not realistically be depended upon. It had to be reinforced with friendly encounters if it were to promote genuine solidarity and thus serve as support in dangerous times. Alternatively, kinship networks might be replaced entirely by networks of friends who were not connected by blood. This fact is confirmed in several of the sagas: friendship alliances are built; friends help each other through political and social difficulties.

If the sagas' formulations on friends and friendship are collated, it becomes apparent that friendship is something that requires action. Occasionally friendship is presented a bald fact, merely existing in an unchanging situation, but more often the sagas treat it as something to be won, or to be confirmed with gifts and favors. It is vulnerable at the same time as it saves lives. Friends give advice and gifts, help each other, confide in each other, come to terms for each other, and do not fight each other. To a degree this picture is determined by the genre. The crux of the sagas' narratives is the potential enmity between strong men, after all. The intrigue revolves around how a looming conflict can be handled without open feud. To this end, alliances are formed that are vital not only when the fighting begins, but also before, when hostilities are dealt with by negotiation and *ting* decisions. What Jesse Byock calls "advocacy" is central in the chain of quarrel, arbitration, and settlement that constitutes the narrative's dramatic structure; it means that influential men are called upon to treat on behalf of a good friend.[26]

Perhaps the most beautiful—although in the end tragic—example of a firm friendship, without any family affiliation, is described in *Njal's Saga*, that masterpiece of terse dramatic narration. Njal is a wise and cautious man, well read in the law, and generally respected in official matters. The other leading character in the saga, his friend Gunnar, is introduced with a flattering list of his many capabilities. He can swing a sword and throw a spear with either hand, and he can jump more than his own height in full armor. As if that was not enough, the saga tells us he can swim like a seal. He is said to be handsome, with fair skin, blue eyes, a straight nose, ruddy cheeks, and a fine head of hair. The description ends: 'He was extremely well-bred, fearless, generous, and even-tempered, faithful to his friends but careful in his choice of them. He was prosperous.'[27]

Both Njal and Gunnar are certainly splendid men, although in different ways. Njal is older, calmer, and wiser. Gunnar is bolder, stronger, and more handsome. Both, however, try to keep their peace, avoid conflict, and choose their friends with care. On one occasion, Njal helps Gunnar with food and fodder. The saga tells us:

> Njal said, 'Here is some hay and food I want to give you. And I want you to turn to me and never to anyone else if ever you find yourself in need.'
>
> 'Your gifts are good,' said Gunnar, 'but I value even more highly your true friendship and that of your sons.'
>
> With that Njal returned home. The spring wore on.[28]

The fatal flaw is that Gunnar has been less than lucky in his choice of wife. She is beautiful but envious and hot-tempered, and she tends to provoke and insult everyone whom she encounters. It is because of her that Gunnar is faced with endless quarrels and bitter disputes. To the very last he tries to solve his problems by legal means, through conciliation in the *ting*. He has Njal's good advice to fall back on, and his friends to assist him. But it cannot be helped. In the end, both he and Njal die in violent fights on account of their mutual solidarity, while their kindred have become bitter enemies. Friendship is not just for fun, it is a matter of life and death.

The relationship between Njal and Gunnar shows that voluntary friendship networks could be more important than blood ties in Icelandic mediaeval culture. Family solidarity is actually jeopardized in *Njal's Saga*. The friendship between the two leading characters is so strong, so morally superior, that it even survives the conflict between their wives and kin.

Generally speaking, friendship in the Icelandic sagas, much like patronage, has little to do with the joy of seeing each other or enjoying a good meal together. It was a much more serious affair. It referred to a broader social context. Friendship mattered whenever there was a semi-political or legal meeting, whenever armies met in the field. Friendship alliances, like other social alliances, were the very breath of life for the mediaeval Icelanders of the sagas. They were necessary if only because a harsh climate and endless natural disasters made it difficult for people to survive. There was no king and no state organization. It was down to individuals to build up networks to guarantee their personal security, to pursue important cases in the *ting*, or to forestall unnecessary conflicts by bringing in influential friends to mediate on their behalf. The concept of cronyism simply did not exist in the Icelandic sagas; the very essence of friendship was helping a friend in any way possible, even at risk of life and limb.

Virtually every family saga is about alliances; built, broken, patched together again, extended, or shrunk, all to make it possible to pursue the protagonist's case successfully in the *ting* or to obtain his rights by force of arms. This is why men forge bonds, harp on ties of kinship or friendship, and give or keep promises—but they do not do so lightly. Lives are at stake.

There are also many passages about friendship in *Hávamál*, "the Lay of the High One," in the Poetic Edda written down in the thirteenth century. As Aron Gurevich says, *Hávamál* should be read as a collection of practical advice on how the individual should behave in order to function in society.[29] Much of the advice in the poem concerns vigilance and caution. It is important not to be insulted or to insult anyone else, not to be deceived, not to behave so that people lose their respect for you, not offend your friends and make enemies of them. The world of the *Hávamál* is a dangerous one. That is precisely why a man must have friends on whom he can rely. Friendship in the verses is not based on emotion but on utility. You should give friends gifts and do them favors in order to receive gifts and favors in return. Friendship is not a goal in life but a means, a means that makes life possible, not least in the public sphere.

Friendship as threat and support

In the Middle Ages there was much profound reflection on friendship by Christian thinkers, as I have shown. Likewise there was the laconic but equally vital tradition of friendship in prose form, for example in the Icelandic sagas. Both were somewhat different from the friendship we recognize today. According to modern norms, friendship is something private to be protected from society at large, something we enjoy when we withdraw from public life for rest and recreation. This, as I have argued, is at odds with Aristotle's philosophy of friendship, where public life ought to profit from the friends' ability to be just and wise, and to concur with each other, that was instilled in them in an ideal friendship.

Mediaeval Christian thought adopted the classical idea that perfect friendship was not an end in itself, but rather a means to achieve something nobler. In the perfect spiritual friendship, each friend was the other's *custos animi*. The friends guarded each other's souls as they trod their shared path to God.

Yet where friendship did not measure up to the Christian ideal, on the other hand, the Church authorities regarded it as a source of danger. It could tempt individuals to do wrong. Moreover, friendship could be considered a threat if there was a risk it would distract those in orders into giving priority to one or two special friends rather than the spiritual collective—or even to secular friends outside the monastery.

Meanwhile, Iceland in the Middle Ages offers a remarkably clear-cut case of a peasant society that lacked both king and state. In the absence of a central political power, such social integration depended on the existence of laws and the *ting* where men could negotiate to achieve justice and concord. In the sagas' world, friendship was not only beneficial, supplying the individual with protection and gifts. It was also absolutely necessary—in private as well as in public life. Similar to ties of blood and marriage, or upbringing in the case of foster-brothers, friendship was an alliance that could promote social, legal, and semi-political goals. It was a serious and largely public matter. This is precisely why it also entailed risk. As in *Njal's Saga*, the bonds of amity could very easily be drowned in blood.

Friendship in the early modern period

It is not hard to find examples of important friendship networks in the early modern period too, in public as well as private life. In Renaissance Italy, for example, merchants engaged in long-distance commerce had for long periods to rely on their partners in foreign countries, since communications were slow and precarious. Ultimately they had to establish friendly relations with their partners to be able to trust them.[30] Friendship also mattered tremendously in the elite social circles of early modern Europe, be it France, England or Sweden, as has been demonstrated by numerous historians.[31] The nobility travelled all over Europe armed with letters of personal recommendation from their friends to open the way to positions in universities, armies, or royal courts. Recent research in England has revealed dynamic friendship networks in wider commercial and cultural exchanges on the part of clergymen and merchants.[32]

Sometimes, friendship was far closer to a patron–client relationship than it was to an ideal friendship, however much it was framed in the rhetoric of friendship. While it was still informal and characterized by reciprocity and trust, it also had an obvious hierarchical dimension. The patron helped his client and talked to him as a friend, but when all was said and done he was nevertheless the one in command. Patronage lacked the quality of equality, of parity, so important to the classical philosophy of ideal friendship. In any event, friendship continued to transcend the dividing line between private and public life in the early modern period, either as patronage veiled in the language of friendship or as true friendship between equals.

In point of fact, the early modern period—and not least the seventeenth and eighteenth centuries—has been called a golden age of friendship. Friendship had a central place in people's outlook, and its vocabulary was used across a broad social spectrum, applied to relationships that were horizontal and vertical, equal and hierarchical.

An expert on English literature, Laurie Shannon, makes the case that friendship permeated Shakespeare's day, the late sixteenth century and early seventeenth. Friendship transcended the boundary between private and public, which gave it a certain utopian potential. The differences between poor and rich in reality were vast, as were the contrasts between the educated elite and the agrarian majority with their oral culture. Even within the same social class, the nobility for example, there were enormous variations. The king's closest adviser and his youngest page did not meet on the same level even if they both came from good families. Even so, most held that friendship should be built on equality, or at any rate on aspirations to equality. Talk of friendship could thus stir up the hope that it might be possible to realize a relationship that was not hierarchical. The idea that a friend could be a second self—evident on stage and in reality—conjured up an alternative order that did not yet exist. Equality and consent suggested a political vision that ran directly counter to the existing, hierarchical status quo.[33]

In fiction, according to Shannon, friendship was often even more important than the love between man and woman. It is possible that in her enthusiasm Shannon overstates the "sovereignty of friendship" because of its prominence in the subtle double-dealings of Shakespeare's dramas. But we cannot deny her point that fiction in the seventeenth century was to a large extent fixated on friendship. For authors in Shakespeare's day, ideal friendship between equals was a trope that challenged the condescension of the tyrants towards their subjects.[34]

As we have seen, Shannon supports her argument primarily with examples drawn from fiction. As a historian, however, one cannot help but wonder what less well-read men and women thought; the people who were not Shakespeare, who did not even see his plays, but worked in their shops or on their farms, marched to war when they were ordered, or paid court to the country's highest officials; but also those who had political power by the standards of the day. In other words, it is a matter of finding the evidence of friendship, of seeking out talk of friendship in source material other than literature. How did people who were not poets put their thoughts on friends and friendship into words in the early modern period? Did such terms as friendship and friend belong to official, political language, or only to private converse?

A political term

In analyses of early modern Scandinavian material it is apparent that friendship was a significant term in the political and judicial spheres. It was not only a word that belonged in everyday talk about individual relationships. For example, Bo H. Lindberg has shown how in eighteenth-century jurisprudence, friendship was interwoven with ideas of an ethic derived from virtue. Church and State wanted citizens who acted from duty, virtue, and friendship. Enmity, meanwhile, was associated with hate, hostility, and violence. This idea can be clearly seen in legal sentencing in the seventeenth and eighteenth centuries. If a man accused of duelling could show that he was in fact a good friend of his adversary, it influenced both the judgement and the punishment. Friendship indicated that the accused was not a wicked man who had planned to attack his victim in an act of cold-blooded revenge. The result was that the judges might well take a more indulgent view of what had occurred. In other words, friendship was a key term in ethics, politics, and law.[35]

The word friendship also served in the high politics of the seventeenth century to signal peaceful relations and alliances. I have considered this in the light of the diplomatic activities of Sweden's famed Queen Christina in the middle of the seventeenth century, before she shocked Europe by abdicating and converting to Catholicism. As monarch she conducted a brisk diplomacy in her attempt to bring peace after the long and costly Swedish engagement in the European wars. Christina (1626–1689) was Gustavus Adolphus's daughter, and inherited all the problems an expansive foreign policy had brought to Sweden.

In 1645, for example, the Peace of Brömsebro was concluded between Sweden and Denmark, in which

Sweden made considerable territorial gains. Christina had good reason to command that services of thanksgiving be held across the country. In such proclamations, she spoke directly to her subjects about what had happened and what was imminent, what they should hope for and what they should fear, and how the realm stood united under monarch and God.[36] It is instructive to look more closely at how this message of war and peace was formulated for its audience:

> Thus was broached cruel and bloody war between Sweden, our beloved Fatherland, and Denmark, and on both sides hosts arrayed in enmity to do bloodshed, even now happily ceased and stayed, and an enduring peace and friendship between Us and him in these Nordic Realms was established and confirmed.[37]

War is characterised as cruel and bloody, peace as enduring and analogous to friendship. In the same proclamation the Queen expressed her fond hope that there would be peace in Germany, where Swedish troops were still fighting. A few months earlier she had reflected on the wars. It is now fifteen years since her beloved father was forced to intervene against the Holy Roman Emperor to save his co-religionists, she begins. Now the Queen has ascended her throne. She hopes that God in his mercy will give her forces success so that there will be peace, and friendship will reign between Sweden and her neighbors. And yet, she laments, God has not seen fit to free the country of the visitations of war, and instead is punishing the Swedes with two concurrent wars. Not only have the Swedish troops long been embroiled in the complex conflicts in Germany; now Denmark in turn has forced a new war upon Sweden.[38] In the royal bill presented to the parliament of 1651, Christina speaks of how she is intent on friendship and trust, blessed peace and amity with other powers.[39] One year on she expounded at some length on the blessings of the prevailing peace after all the years of war that had afflicted the realm both at home and abroad. There is all the more reason to thank God for this "supreme happiness" of peace, she says, for the like was not before seen in her or her parents' day, nor in other countries in Europe.[40] Prior to her abdication in 1654, she ascribed to God and to herself the honor of concluding the peace. She has been at pains to be a "good friend" to Sweden's neighbors.

Thus it is through God's munificence and Her Royal Majesty's tender care in these dangerous times, and the war and its dangers that beset us from all sides, thus far to vouchsafe us to reside in peace and safety, keeping us from being drawn in to other's quarrels and tribulations. To that end Her Royal Majesty has endeavoured to maintain and cultivate with her neighbors and near nations all good friendship and sound reason.[41]

Whereupon Christina runs through all Sweden's important international relations, pointing out the "good friendship" that already exists, or failing that at least the existence of a truce and ongoing dialogue.[42] The wars are described throughout as a punishment from God. They are cruel and bloody, and signify "enmity." The key attributes of peace are that it brings safety, peace, and good repute, and its synonyms are constructed using "friendship": the usual phrases are "friendship and alliance," "peace and friendship," "friendship and trust," "friendship and accord." Where there is peace between nations, there is trust between them, and friendship. Friendship thus not only signals a relationship within an individual's private circle, it also applies in public life, just as in the classical theory of friendship and mediaeval political alliances. Indeed, it constitutes a central element in the political language of the day. In high politics, friendship signifies peaceful contacts, mutual trust, and the absence of conflict.[43]

How then to interpret this? Official documents such as these crystallize the government's views on the international and domestic situation, presented at a specific, solemn occasion. It goes without saying that the texts amount to a separate genre, whether you interpret them as clever rhetoric used to motivate new burdens being placed on the people, as an authoritative history, or as a genuine attempt to create social order and a sense of community. Unsurprisingly, given the circumstances, the texts are distinguished by their degree of abstraction and dignity; this was not the place to heap curses on the heads of incompetent office-holders or the military, no more than it was to give a detailed and repellent account of the true face of war. And it was reasonable for a ruler, in the middle of a war, to set out to persuade the populace that the war was necessary for the good of the realm, even if peace was really the ultimate, and most desirable, end. How otherwise would people manage, how could they endure it? The official documents need to give a viable argument for both war and peace. At the same time they refer to the doctrine of the just war that had been developing since the Middle Ages.[44] References to friendship fitted well with the solemn religious and political rhetoric. They allude to classical ideals and Christian ethics, while at the same time they suggest the joy and happiness of people's everyday social existence. In my view it is on this very duality that friendship's strength as a discourse depends. For the populace, talk of friends and friendship was intelligible, and for the educated conjured up classical teaching and centuries of ethical and philosophical reflection. The language of friendship could roam freely across the boundaries between private and public.

In early modern politics, friendship thus meant peaceful contact, mutual trust, and an absence of conflict. Its opposites were violence, war, or betrayal; its counterparts, negotiation, consideration, and peace. It was clearly understood that wherever friendship and trust reigned, whenever negotiations were afoot, violence was absent. Wherever violence struck, friendship did not, could not, exist.[45]

A noblewoman, a clergyman, and a merchant—and their friends

Friendship and friends were integral to seventeenth-century political and literary idiom, as we have seen. But official pronouncements and poetry are one thing. Reality is another. How can we find out what people's real lives with their friends were like? Whom did they count as friends, and what did these relationships mean to them? Surviving correspondence and diaries can come to the historian's rescue. Let us consider a few examples. I will begin with my own study of Swedish material, moving on to discuss the observations of other historians from English material.

There are precious few large collections of correspondence surviving in Sweden from the period before the eighteenth century, especially if we step outside the circles of famous statesmen. But there are a number of glorious exceptions. Take the down-to-earth and indiscreet letters written by Catharina Wallenstedt throughout a long life that spanned most of the seventeenth century. Catharina was born in 1627 and died in 1719, at what for the period was the remarkably advanced age of 92. She was the daughter of a cathedral dean in Uppsala. He later became bishop of Strängnäs, and the family was ennobled, taking the name Wallenstedt. Catharina received a good upbringing at home, and spent some time at Queen Christina's court. In time she married Edvard Philipsson, he too from a clerical family. He was ennobled in his turn, and was sent overseas on the king's business. The couple had several children.

Catharina often remained at home in Sweden to care for the children and the household while her husband was abroad. In due course her sons left to make their way in the world, several of them as military officers.

Over 350 letters from Catharina Wallenstedt's hand survive. They provide an unmatched opportunity to reconstruct her daily life and values, but also the world of gossip, court intrigue, war, disease, and poor harvests that she and so many others were forced to live through. It is touching to see her concern when her sons go out to war like so many other young men around her.[46] It is also apparent from the letters how Catharina Wallenstedt fought for her family's honor and status. She courts the most powerful members of society to obtain favors for family members. She asks her husband to send home beautiful jewellery, clothes, and furniture so that the family can maintain their status with their possessions, very much in keeping with seventeenth-century luxury consumption.[47] She does her duty for the family within the parameters of the patron–client system of the day, in which paying suit and personal persuasion were crucial ingredients.[48]

What do the letters tell us about the friendships of an upper-class seventeenth-century lady? I have consulted her letters from a period of nearly fifty years, from 1672 to 1718, with a particular eye to what Catharina says about love, friends, and friendship. Naturally we cannot reconstruct her entire social life from her letters to her husband, children, and grandchildren. Correspondence is always selective, tailored to what we want to communicate and what the addressee wants to know. Nor is it possible to extract qualitative information of any significance from any such analysis. What we can ask, however, is whether Catharina Wallenstedt was discriminating or generously inclusive when it came to naming people as her friends. Did she draw a line between friends and relations, between close friends and acquaintances? Was she alert to the difference, as historians today would see it, between a relationship of an obviously self-seeking character (of the patron–client mould) and a relationship based on faith placed in individuals whom you have known long, share memories with, and trust?

Catharina Wallenstedt's way of writing about her friends and relatives displays an interesting ambiguity. She is without doubt given to reflection. She knows her way around the alliance system in which the words friend and friendship could be invoked for outright gain. It was favors done and returned, but also an agreeable culture of conviviality, that upheld the patron–client. At the same time, however, there were friends and friendships of a completely different caliber in Catharina's world. These were the friends who never failed to visit her, who always enquired after her and her family's health, who asked for her help when there was a death in their family or for her advice when their children were sick. In fact, it is these people whom Catharina herself explicitly calls her friends. They are few in number: in the whole of Catharina's long life perhaps only between seven and ten, judging by the letters. It is obvious that Catharina herself distinguished between acquaintances and 'real' friends. Amongst her friends she included a couple of people to whom she was related. But by no means all her kin, including close relatives, enjoyed her favor. Most of her friends were women: the wives or widows of men who were old friends of the family, or in a couple of instances neighbors. They were women who found themselves in a similar situation as Catharina herself, and came from much the same social circles; their husbands were senior military men or government office-holders.

Other examples of the discourse and practice of friendship in the seventeenth and eighteenth centuries can be drawn from international research. The anthropologist Alan Macfarlane's analysis of Ralph

Josselin's social networks provides many interesting insights. Ralph Josselin was born in Essex in England in 1617 and died the vicar of Earls Colne in 1683. He kept a diary for much of his life. With its help and other sources it is possible to reconstruct his finances, social life, and thoughts. Alan Macfarlane's study is packed with information about family and relatives, births, debt, religion, and politics. His primary focus is Josselin's family and relatives—unsurprisingly given that the book was written at a time when anthropologists and cultural historians had not yet shown any real interest in friendship—and only in passing does he discuss Josselin's friendships.

Josselin's diaries show that in such circles, people who married into a family were often called friends; they were not as close as blood relatives, but were still closer than neighbors, who did not automatically become friends. You could not choose your neighbors, after all. That Josselin attached great importance to the fact that real friends were chosen is apparent when he writes with great sorrow about a close female friend's death. She had been as friendly and loving as a sister, and was "my deare friend ... a choyce speciall friend." The friend in question, the spinster Mary Church, had given Josselin and his family numerous gifts, and ultimately bequeathed a considerable sum to them. In other words, the relationship had financial significance for Josselin, but that did not prevent it from being built on genuine affection. It is clear in the diaries who belonged to Josselin's small circle of close friends, writes Macfarlane. Mary Church was one, as were Master and Mistress Elliston. The families were always together, and helped one another. Amongst his friends Josselin could also count the wealthy families in the district who often gave him advice and financial assistance.

The conclusions to be drawn from Josselin's diaries are interesting in several ways. On the one hand it seems Josselin called both relatives and patrons friends. On the other, it is clear that he set his own boundaries for whom he wanted to view as a real friend, just as Catharina Wallenstedt did. His little circle of good friends may well have included people from whom he would have drawn an obvious benefit. Yet real friendship for Josselin was still a form of profound reciprocity, expressed in gifts and thoughtfulness. Besides, he himself emphasizes how true friendship is built on voluntary, mutual exchange and the empathy of souls.[49] Josselin's reflections are in fact quite close to Aristotle's and Cicero's ideas.

In another thought-provoking book on family and friendship in England in the eighteenth century, the

Israeli–British historian Naomi Tadmor has traced the use of the words 'friend' and 'friendship' in texts of the period. The objective of the book is an analysis of what was then termed friendship, and of the people in an individual's circle who were termed friends. At its heart is some truly remarkable source material. Over one hundred autobiographical notebooks have survived from the period 1754–1765, kept by a merchant by the name of Thomas Turner. Naomi Tadmor starts with the assumption that Turner knew what he meant when he used the word friend in his diaries. Nor does she think there is any reason to believe that he was unique in his understanding, but rather that he reflects the thoughts and decisions that were usual in his day. Tadmor also studies other material such as educational tracts and popular novels.[50] Her frame of reference, methods, and interpretations strike me as convincing.

She is looking for what one might call the language of emotions in close relationships. She follows Turner's use of the words friend and friendship, but also how he defines the boundaries of family and household. An important point is that Turner's understanding of family primarily revolved around the household. The household-family was in turn based on cohabitation, and on the recognition by all who lived in the same house of the authority of the head of the household. For Thomas Turner, blood relations—or rather, at least one blood relation—played an important role. But his definition of family stretched to include everyone who lived in his house, even if their function was more that of apprentice.[51] The household was the functional unit in daily life. You could call your sister-in-law, your half-sister, or your wife's sister all "sister," it appears. Applying the word for close relatives (sisters or brothers) to other relationships under the same roof was a way of marking affinity. The language of kinship was thus used not only to describe relationships determined by blood or marriage, but also to reproduce social connections and mutual obligations in a slightly wider circle.[52]

How then do the words friend and friendship relate to the other words in the language of close relationships? The designations friend and friendship are for Turner inclusive terms. Even so, he was both precise and discriminating in his use of the epithet friend. To be counted Turner's friend you had to occupy one or more of the following positions: you were one of Turner's relatives; you shared an intellectual affinity with him; you were a trustworthy merchant with whom he had worked closely; you were his tenant; you were a government officer who was important to him or one of his political friends. At the heart of all the talk of friendship, writes Tadmor, we find the word 'service.' There was in other words a degree of instrumentality in Turner's manner of speaking about friends and friendship. But Tadmor's point is that utility and pure feelings do not necessarily exclude each other. She maintains that friendship was a complex business: the relationships were affective and sentimental, but also instrumental.[53]

In the eighteenth century the term friend had a variety of meanings that spanned kinship, financial ties, professional contacts, intellectual and spiritual connections, social networks, and political alliances. Amongst Thomas Turner's "friends" his wife Peggy was to his mind the most important. The relationship between spouses was at that time expressed as a moral relationship, as a friendship. Turner himself reflects on his marriage in his diary entry for 1 January 1756: he was drawn into marriage, he writes, not from greed or lust, but from nothing other than "the Pure and desirable Sake of Friendship."[54] When Peggy died, Turner expressed his grief using the terminology of friendship; he had lost his "sincere friend." He mourned no longer having a "friend" who could calm his fears, someone with whom he could spend an hour together in "holy friendship."[55]

After a systematic analysis of the diaries, Tadmor concludes that the number of people in Turner's diary who are called "friend" and at the same time were not relatives comes to a total of sixteen. All were men. Two were schoolteachers, several were merchants, one was a doctor, and some were public officers. They formed a male network that had one foot in the private sphere and one in the public. They combined utility with pleasure. Such friendship networks left women firmly excluded. His wife may have been an exception, but she was a friend in a different sense.[56]

Turner certainly viewed friendship as a relationship voluntarily entered into, preferably between equals. Yet the way he used the word friend indicates that he had a much broader underlying definition. Both relatives and non-relatives could be included in his friendship network, business contacts as well as more private friends. Friendship was enacted not only in the private sphere, but also in the public sphere.[57]

Naomi Tadmor finds further support for her argument in early modern English philosophical texts on friendship, particularly Jeremy Taylor's *The Measures and Offices of Friendship* (1662). Taylor wrestled with classical and mediaeval ideas about friendship: here the Christian dilemma of bringing together universal charity and an exclusive personal relationship: there Aristotle's ideas of the different types of friendship—natural, beneficial, pleasurable, and virtuous. Taylor thought that they were intermixed. Natural relationships (between siblings or spouses) could very well become the best friendships. While it is true that there was a preference for choosing new, unrelated people as friends, it was just as reasonable for natural relationships occasionally to be subsumed into friendship, for people to choose their friends from their existing kin. Friendship as a relationship was therefore composite: it was natural and contractual, elective and predetermined, equal and hierarchal. For Taylor, friendship was in essence practical and did not flinch from being instrumental. Yet friendship also tried to adhere to the ethical principles of virtue and religion.[58]

The degree of uncertainty in the early modern period about which people living together could be counted as members of a household, does not according to Naomi Tadmor necessarily signify that people were unclear about who constituted their closest family or who was their best friend. There were countless ways of marking the differences. In Britain, relatives could be called "natural friends," as distinct from other "friends." Both business contacts and childhood neighbors could be called friends. But equally, people were more than capable of differentiating between friends and friends, kith and kin.

Judging by the surviving correspondence and other private material, talk of friendship in the seventeenth and eighteenth centuries was thus characterized by both inclusiveness and the ability to make distinctions. The noblewoman Catharina Wallenstedt, the clergyman Ralph Josselin, and the merchant Thomas Turner all spoke of certain close relatives—although not all of them—as friends. They had a variety of friendships, but clearly differentiated between really good friends and more fleeting acquaintances. This meant that they implicitly placed demands on the people who merited to be named friend. Real friends, after all, were rather more than acquaintances to be courted to achieve specific ends. Meanwhile, the giving and receiving of favors was a part of the social pattern not only in hierarchical patron-client contacts but also in the horizontal connections of friendship.

The idea that friendship should spring from free choice, and should be characterized by trust and reciprocity, seems to have been clear to everyone, whether they had read classical philosophy or not. On the other hand, the practice of friendship in the early modern period seems often to have been devoid of the equality demanded by ideal friendship; it is at any rate sometimes difficult for later observers to distinguish in early modern sources between hierarchical patron–client relationships and the ideal friendship of relative equals. The observation that friendship was not seen as something to be restricted to private life seems once again born out.

The dangers of cronyism

The early modern period saw the acceleration of state-formation in Europe. Much interesting research has focused on the differences between the early modern state and the weaker power networks of the Middle Ages. Several historians have followed in Weber and Elias' footsteps to emphasize the advent of bureaucratic rules, financial controls, and a state monopoly on violence as crucial elements in early modern state-formation.[59] Others have argued that early control systems were far from perfect, and that the State long remained an organization dependent on networks of local actors and entrepreneurs to achieve order and stability.[60]

Whichever is correct, there is general agreement that in most countries in Europe the early modern period saw an attempt to improve the legal framework of government and the competence of public servants. Formal education and professional training thus gradually make their appearance. In principle this should have undermined the importance of informal contacts, friendship alliances, and patron–client relationships in public life. For a long time, though, the two existed in parallel: bureaucracy and meritocracy on the one hand, personal loyalty on the other. The combination was typical for the period, and it was a neither irrational nor inept approach to handling the state's problems. Natalie Zemon Davis, for example, has stressed the particular rationality of social networks in early modern France. The state and its representatives, looking for skilled men to fulfill official duties, might well be critical of individual candidates who tried to use their networks, but they seem often to have accepted both social contacts and other skills as being the right combination of merits.[61]

Turning our attention to Sweden, long recognized as one of the best examples of effective state-formation in the early modern period, it is clear that the

State claimed a monopoly on the armed forces and the administration of justice, while successfully establishing a relatively strong central bureaucracy and a fiscal system of sorts. In the process, informal social networks in the public sphere—which operated through friendships—were challenged and sometimes openly criticized. As early as the sixteenth century the king's chief adviser, Olaus Petri, was quick to argue that a judge, in his professional capacity, should be careful to set aside his own personal loyalties. Should he fail to do so, and the sentence he handed down was biased or showed signs of being corrupted by friendship, then he would have lost his honor and be utterly disgraced. Step by step, the state introduced laws and oaths in which friendship was defined as a potential corruptor of public life, much like kinship, bribery, or faction; a development that was first most apparent in the courts.

Prohibitions against interference with witnesses in court cases, whether suborned by friendship or enmity, are constantly repeated in different Swedish edicts, particularly in the seventeenth century. The need for repetition itself demonstrates the extent of cronyism, what in Swedish is called literally "friendship corruption." The state was aware that friendship networks and patron–client relationships could influence people to take sides in a way that might jeopardize justice. It was for this reason that particular emphasis was placed on dangers of bias in legal proceedings, and that such situations should be avoided if at all possible. In legislation on the Swedish navy from 1667, for example, it was stipulated that partial witnesses should be avoided, "that for friendship of the one party, and enmity of the other, they can be suspected of not being neutral; and therefore they may not bear witness." In the army ordinances of 1683, it was laid down that witnesses should swear an oath in which they promised not to let friendship, affinity, envy, hate, or gifts determine their testimony. Similarly, the Swedish General Law of 1734 demanded that all witnesses involved in a trial had to swear to tell the truth and nothing but the truth, neither should they keep silent about anything relevant to the case, be it for friendship, kinship, gifts, threats, promises, and so on, "so help me God." This has been the model for all similar oaths in Sweden ever since.[62]

So, according to the representatives of public life, personal friends might corrupt the administration of justice, or indeed any other civil or military business. In the Europe of the seventeenth and eighteenth centuries, where war was more common than peace, monarchs and high state officials began increasingly to demand military competence from their armed forces, achieved by formal education and training. It was no longer enough for a young nobleman to have famous relatives and influential friends, although it is true that education combined with the right contacts seems to have been irresistible. For example, in the middle of the eighteenth century, the nobleman Axel von Fersen was colonel of the Royal-Suédois regiment in France. When he recruited new officers to his regiment, he paid particular attention to whether the applicant came from a noble family and had influential personal contacts. However, it has also been shown that he was equally interested in the candidate's experience, competence, and formal education. Having good friends in the right places was not enough for the armies or diplomatic corps of the day. Theirs was a friendship-based culture, but they were none the less alert to the risks of friendship in public life. The ambition of judging merit and competence on objective grounds had by this time been fully adopted.[63]

With the advent of effective state-formation, and even more so in the nineteenth and twentieth centuries when modernization coalesced with democracy and welfare, patronage and networks—of friends and kin alike—lost something of their charm in public life. Instead, formal instructions and written rules, the principles of unbiased meritocracy and rational bureaucracy, increasingly characterized public life. In the process, at least on a discursive and normative level, friendship was explicitly defined as an informal relationship that belonged firmly in the private sphere.

Private and public—hierarchical and equal

To summarize, then, even if all societies and periods have seen a dividing line between *res publica* and *res privata*, the public and private spheres, this line has not always been drawn in the same way. Moreover, there have always been relationships, ideas, and phenomena that have transcended or blurred the same dividing line. I have argued that friendship, as a discourse and a practice, is one such phenomenon, for it existed both in the private and public spheres from classical antiquity through the Middle Ages to the early modern period. This is in stark contrast to the idea prevalent in the twentieth century that friendship was primarily a private concern.

Aristotle, one of the great classical philosophers of friendship, was an early advocate of the view that, in ideal circumstances, friendship could inspire virtue and excellence, bestowing ethical and political qualities that had bearing on the state of society at large. By the same token, he was certain that friendships were more than a matter of mutual advantage or pleasure.

That friendship could transcend the boundary between private and public; that it might be good for the friends in question: these were ideas that survived into the mediaeval and early modern periods. The dangers of mediaeval society and its uncertain configuration of power forced people to seek their own alliances in order to survive. This was as true of farmers as it was of noblemen. Some alliances were based on kinship, but modern research now increasingly emphasizes that ties of friendship also constituted primary alliances. I have illustrated this with cases in point from the Icelandic sagas. In the early modern period the language of friendship was used both in political discourse and in the relationships between the patrons and clients who thronged the corridors of public life. But equally we can see from diaries and correspondence that merchants, clergymen, and noblewomen were quite capable of differentiating between their real friends and instrumental acquaintances.

Mediaeval thinkers had a problem in harnessing classical ideas of ideal friendship to a Christian ideology in which loyalty to the Church and the individual's search for God should not be hindered by a private relationship between two friends. It was for this reason that friendship was periodically seen as a threat in the Middle Ages, even as a Christian version of ideal friendship was gradually articulated in the idea of spiritual friendship as a stage on the path to God.

The early modern period also identified a major problem with friendship, this time when the state took a firmer grip on the public administration, economy, and judiciary. Friendship could at worst degenerate into cronyism, with its corollaries in the perversion of justice and the appointment of incompetents to high office. Taking examples from Sweden, I have demonstrated how the state slowly introduced increasing numbers of laws and ordinances that defined friendship as a threat to the execution of justice.

The criteria for defining friendship that were suggested by our classical forebears—reciprocity, trust, voluntariness, and equality—all recur in the discourses of the mediaeval and early modern periods. But equality was more often a Utopia, a compelling vision, than a reality. When friendship crossed the line between private and public, it was often as a relationship that was hierarchical rather than equal.

81

Notes

[1] Jürgen Habermas, *The Structural Transformation of the Public Sphere: An Inquiry into a Category of Bourgeois Society*, trans. T. Burger & F. Lawrence, Cambridge, 1989 (1st ed. 1962).

[2] Naomi Tadmor, "Revisiting the public sphere and the history of the family," in Kenneth Johansson & Marie Lindstedt Cronberg, eds., *Vänskap över gränser: en festskrift till Eva Österberg*, Lund, 2007, p. 217.

[3] See, for example, Peter Aronsson, *Bönder gör politik: Det lokala självstyret som social arena i tre smålandssocknar*, Lund, 1992; Eva Österberg, "State Formation and the People: The Swedish Model in Perspective," in Heinrich R. Schmidt, André Holenstein & Andreas Wurgler, eds., *Gemeinde, Reformation und Widerstand*, Tübingen, 1998.

[4] Georges Duby, "Introduction," in Philippe Ariès & Georges Duby, eds., *A History of Private Life: II. Revelations of the Medieval World*, Cambridge, Mass., and London, 1988, pp. 3–29.

[5] Aristotle, *The Nicomachean Ethics*, trans. J. E. C. Welldon. New York, 1987, p. 271.

[6] Ibid., pp. 254–261.

[7] See Eva Österberg, "Vännerna och jaget. Att bli individ tillsammans med andra" in Marie Lindstedt Cronberg & Catharina Stenqvist, eds., *Förmoderna livshållningar. Dygder, värden och kunskapsvägar från antiken till upplysningen*, Lund, 2008, pp. 50–72.

[8] Søren Kierkegaard, *Antingen—eller, ett livsfragment*. Vols. 1–2,

Önneköp, 2002; Paul Ricoeur, *Oneself as Another*, Chicago and London, 1992.

[9] Aristotle, *The Nicomachean Ethics*, pp. 265, 254.

[10] Ronny Ambjörnsson, "En kärlekshistoria" in *Divan 2006: 1–2*. Umeå, 2006; Eva Österberg, *Vänskap—en lång historia*, p. 53.

[11] Cicero, *De senectute, de amicitia, de divinatione*, trans. W. A. Falconer. Cambridge, Mass., 1979, pp. 127, 129, 131, 133, 139, 145, 149, 171, 175–179, 181, 191–193, 197–199, 207.

[12] For the analysis of the classical philosophy of friendship see Eva Österberg, *Vänskap—en lång historia*, pp. 49–69 which includes references to the classical philosophers as well as to modern research.

[13] Eva Österberg, *Vänskap—en lång historia*.

[14] Aron Gurevich, *Medieval popular culture: Problems of belief and perception*, Cambridge, 1988, pp. 1–38.

[15] For a more extended analysis of attitudes towards friendship see Eva Österberg, *Vänskap—en lång historia*, pp. 49–100, 183–218.

[16] Brian McGuire, *Friendship and Community. The Monastic Experience 350–1250*, Kalamazoo, 1988; Eva Österberg, *Vänskap—en lång historia*, p. 55 ff.

[17] Brian McGuire, *Friendship and Community*, pp. 296 ff, 321 ff.

[18] Brian McGuire, *Friendship and Community*; Eva Österberg, *Vänskap—en lång historia*, pp. 55–57, 149–158.

[19] St Birgitta, *Himmelska uppenbarelser*, IV 13, trans. Tryggve Lundén. 1958. My translation.

[20] St Birgitta, *Himmelska uppenbarelser*, IV 126, trans. Tryggve Lundén. 1958, p. 213. My translation.

[21] On the sagas as historical–anthropological source material see, for example, Eva Österberg, *Folk förr*, Stockholm, 1995, pp. 37 ff; Jesse Byock, *Feud in the Icelandic Saga*, Berkeley, 1988; Carol Clover & John Lindow, *Old Norse-Icelandic Literature: A Critical Guide*, Ithaca, 1981; Lars Lönnroth, *Skaldemjödet i berget: Essayer om fornisländsk ordkonst och dess återanvändning i nutiden*, Stockholm 1996; William Ian Miller, *Feud, Law and Society in Saga Iceland*, Ithaca & London, 1990, p. 302; William Ian Miller, *Humiliation: And Other Essays on Honor, Social Discomfort, and Violence*, Ithaca & London 1993; Eva Österberg, "Våldets känslorum: Berättelser om makt och moral i det förmoderna samhället," in Eva Österberg & Marie Lindstedt Cronberg, eds., *Våldets mening: Makt, minne, myt*, Lund, 2004, pp. 19 ff.

[22] E. Paul Durrenberger & Gísli Pálsson, "The Importance of Friendship in the Absence of States, According to the Icelandic Sagas," in S. Bell & S. Kalamazoo, eds., *The Anthropology of Friendship: beyond the Community of Kinship*, Oxford 1999. It should be noted that kinship refers not only to relations by blood but also by marriage.

[23] See Audur Magnúsdóttir, "Kärlekens makt eller maktens kärlek? Om frilloväsende och politik hos Oddaverjarna," conference paper, 1999.

[24] E. Paul Durrenberger & Gísli Pálsson, "The Importance of Friendship," pp. 59–77.

[25] Jón Vidar Sigurdsson, "Friendship in the Icelandic Commonwealth," in Gísli Pálsson, ed., *From Sagas to Society: Comparative Approaches to Early Iceland*, Enfield Lock, 1992, pp. 205–215; Eva Österberg, *Vänskap—en lång historia*, pp. 79–99.

[26] Jesse Byock, *Feud in the Icelandic Saga*, pp. 24 ff, 57 ff, 205 ff. See also Eva Österberg, *Folk förr*, p. 43 ff; and Eva Österberg, "Våldets känslorum," p. 26.

[27] *Njal's saga*, trans. Magnus Magnusson & Hermann Pálsson, chapter 19. London, 1960.

[28] Ibid., chapter 47.

[29] Aron Gurevitj, *Den svårfångade individen*, Stockholm, pp. 43–52.

[30] See, for example, Gunnar Dahl, *Trade, Trust and Networks: Commercial Culture in Late Medieval Italy*, Lund, 1998.

[31] See, for example, Natalie Zemon Davis, *The Gift in Sixteenth-century France*, Oxford, 2000; Fabian Persson, *Servants of Fortune: The Swedish Court between 1598 and 1721*, Lund, 1999.

[32] See, for example, Naomi Tadmor, *Family and Friends in Eighteenth-Century England: Household, Kinship, and Patronage*, Cambridge, 2001.

[33] Laurie Shannon, *Sovereign Amity. Figures of Friendship in Shakespearean Context*, Chicago & London, 2002, pp. 1 ff, 17 ff, 54 ff. 223 ff.

85

[34] Ibid., pp. 1 ff, 11ff, 17 ff, 54 ff, 223 ff.

[35] Bo H. Lindberg, *Praemia et poenae. Etik och straffrätt i Sverige i tidig ny tid*, Uppsala, 1992, pp. 175 ff, 192 ff, 210 ff. For a Lindberg-inspired discussion of dueling as a crime, see Christopher Collstedt, *Duellanten och rättvisan*, Lund, 2007.

[36] On Intercession Day proclamations, see, for example, Elisabeth Reuterswärd, *Ett massmedium för folket. Studier i de allmänna kungörelsernas funktion i 1700-talets samhälle*, Lund, 2001; and Joachim Östlund, *Lyckolandet. Maktens legitimering i officiell retorik från stormaktstid till demokratins genombrott*, 2007. Östlund sees the proclamations as rituals that created communities, and uses them to trace the means by which a form of national identity or social order was created over the course of several centuries.

[37] *Kongl Maj:ts Placat 26 September 1645*, Småtryck, Lunds University Library (hereafter LUB), my translation. For an analysis of Christina's speech, see also Eva Österberg, "Krigens moral och fredens lycka. Kvinnor om våldet på 1600-talet" in Eva Österberg & Marie Lindstedt Cronberg, eds., *Kvinnor och våld. En mångtydig kulturhistoria*, Lund, 2005.

[38] *Kongl Maj:ts Placat om allmänna faste- och bönedagar, 5 March 1645*, Småtryck, LUB, my emphasis. See Eva Österberg, *Vänskap—en lång historia*, pp. 185–192.

[39] *Sveriges Ridderskaps och Adels Riksdags-Protokoll*, 1645–49, p. 605.

86

[40] *Sveriges Ridderskaps och Adels Riksdags-Protokoll* 1652–54, p. 98 ff.

[41] Ibid., p. 282 ff, my translation.

[42] Ibid., pp. 283–284.

[43] See Eva Österberg, *Vänskap—en lång historia*, pp. 185–192. See also Eva Österberg, "Vänskap—hot eller skydd i medeltidens samhälle. En existentiell och etisk historia" in *Historisk tidskrift 2003:4*, Stockholm, 2003, and the literature discussed there; and Eva Österberg, "Våldets känslorum" in Eva Österberg & Marie Lindstedt Cronberg, eds., *Våldets mening. Makt, minne, myt*, Lund, 2004 p. 22 ff. The use of friendship to foster dialogue as part of the attempt to peacefully resolve modern conflicts is demonstrated by Maria Småberg, *Ambivalent friendship. Anglican Conflict-handling and Education for Peace in Jerusalem 1920–1948*, Lund, 2005.

[44] Eva Österberg, "Krigens moral och fredens lycka" in Eva Österberg & Marie Lindstedt Cronberg, eds., *Kvinnor och våld. En mångtydig kulturhistoria*. Lund, 2005, p. 121 ff.

[45] On friendship as self-control and negotiation, and thus the opposite of violence, see Eva Österberg, "Våldets känslorum. Berättelser om makt och moral i det förmoderna samhället," and Kenneth Johansson, "Makt, våld och besinning," both in Eva Österberg & Marie Lindstedt Cronberg, eds., *Våldets mening*.

[46] On Catharina Wallenstedt's correspondence, see Eva

87

Österberg, "På samhällsstegens högsta topp. Drottning eller husfru" in Eva Österberg, ed., *Jämmerdal och fröjdesal: Kvinnor i stormaktstidens Sverige*, Stockholm, 1997 p. 345 ff; and Eva Österberg, "Krigens moral och fredens lycka. Kvinnor om våld på 1600-talet" in Eva Österberg & Marie Lindstedt Cronberg, eds., *Kvinnor och våld*, p. 124 ff.

[47] See Margareta Revera, "En barock historia" in Gudrun Ekstrand, ed., *Tre Karlar: Karl X Gustav, Karl XI, Karl XII.* Stockholm, 1984; and the discussion of the literature in Eva Österberg, "På samhällsstegens högsta topp. Drottning eller husfru," in Eva Österberg, ed., *Jämmerdal och fröjdesal*, p. 334 ff.

[48] Compare, for example, Fabian Persson, *Servants of Fortune. The Swedish Court between 1598 and 1721*, Lund, 1999.

[49] Alan Macfarlane, *The Family Life of Ralph Josselin, a Seventeenth-Century Clergyman: An Essay in Historical Anthropology*, London, 1970, p. 149 ff. See also the discussion in Eva Österberg, *Vänskap—en lång historia*, p. 199 ff.

[50] Naomi Tadmor, *Family and Friends in Eighteenth-Century England*.

[51] Ibid., pp. 22, 27 ff., 33 f., 73 ff.

[52] Ibid., pp. 139ff.

[53] Ibid., pp. 173, 187.

[54] Ibid., pp. 167, 192.

[55] Ibid., p. 195.

[56] Ibid., pp. 196 f, 207.

[57] Ibid., p. 211 ff.

[58] Ibid., p. 237 ff.

[59] See, for example, Charles Tilly, *Coercion, Capital and European States, AD 990–1990*, Oxford, 1990; Michael Mann, "The Autonomous Power of the State: its Origins, Mechanisms and Results," in John A. Hall, ed., *States in History*, Oxford, 1986; Anthony Giddens, *The Nation-state and Violence*. Cambridge, 1985.

[60] See, for example, Michael J. Braddick, *The Nerves of State, Taxation and the Financing of the English State, 1558–1714*, Manchester and New York, 1996; Michael J. Braddick, *State Formation in Early Modern England, c. 1550–1700*, Cambridge, 2000.

[61] Natalie Zemon Davis, *The Gift in Sixteenth-Century France*, Oxford, 2000.

[62] Eva Österberg, *Vänskap—en lång historia*, pp. 170–181; Olaus Petri, *Några allmänna regler där en domare skall sig alldeles efter rätta ...* Stockholm, 1960.

[63] See, for example, Ingvar Elmroth, *För kung och fosterland*, Lund, 1981; Charlotta Wolff, *Vänskap och makt. Den svenska politiska eliten och upplysningstidens Frankrike*. Jyväskylä, 2005, p. 178 ff.

Chapter 3

Me and My Friends

Individuality, friendship, and autobiography from Augustine to Rousseau

The hermeneutics of self

My themes in this chapter are individuality, autobiography, and friendship. The combination of individuality and autobiography is hardly surprising. Autobiographies are usually regarded as the best place for authors to reflect upon themselves as unique persons and lay bare their individuality. Critical voices are heard accusing autobiographers of being egocentric, if not narcissistic and pompous, and dwelling far too long on their subject; less jaundiced observers note the naked self-criticism and humble attitude that some writers reveal in their autobiographies. In any case, with the recently renewed interest in subject-formation—the development of the individual over time—autobiographies have become important sources for historical analysis.

On the other hand, the combination of individuality and autobiography with friendship seems more unexpected. Yet drawing inspiration from the classical philosophy of friendship, as developed by Aristotle and others, it is obvious to me that this particular combination is well worth serious consideration. In classical philosophy, the ideal friendship constituted a means, a method, for excellent men to achieve their true, wise, and noble character, in a manner that was also useful to the civil state. Thus, in a deep dialogue with a friend, each individual would learn to understand his own self. Together, each was involved in a cognitive as well as an ethical process. The friend was a potential other, but a close and trusting "other," not the incongruous or hostile "other." So in the ideal case, friends would express their individuality with each other, taking part in a kind of moral–political education, which at the same time could only make them useful in a wider social sphere.

In mediaeval Christian thought, however, the discourse on friendship was more ambiguous, as I argued in the previous chapter. It was not a general assumption that the self-reflexive individual would develop to greater effect by conversing with a few close friends. Indeed, some Church authorities held that deeper self-reflection was only possible when the individual was in complete solitude, while others gave priority to the collective life of a religious community.

My task here, then, will be to discuss the following issues:

> To what extent can we identify a process of increased individuality, a potential rise of the individual, in a period spanning from the Middle Ages to modernity?

> Can we observe any such changes when we contrast a few famous autobiographies from European history, starting with Augustine in the Middle Ages, and taking Rousseau in the Enlightenment as the final example? What are the differences and the similarities between their level of self-examination and their expressions of individuality?

> To what extent do these autobiographies deal with friends and friendship as a part of the writer's self-reflection? Is friendship included as a means or as a result of individual development? In what way do the writers focus on friends in their narratives?

My contribution, then, is to ask whether profound reflections on the self have been matched by similar reflections on friendship. Has the "other," in the sense of a friend, been considered important for the individual in his search for greater insight into his own nature? Are self-examination and the autonomy of the subject furthered by a mutual exchange of confidences between close friends?

The contrast between premodern and modern is integral to many generalized models in social and political science when it comes to societal development in Europe, as I have already discussed in chapter 1. Thus we find *premodern* man, who is supposedly characterized by both the idea and the social practice of collectivism, in which the individual had little freedom to choose, and lacked the gift of profound self-reflection. According to such models, premodern man looked to the past and was bound by tradition, including a religious and magic culture. In his social practices, he depended on his local community and his kin. *Modern* man, on the other hand, supposedly possesses reflexivity, autonomy, and a distinct identity as an individual. He looks to the future with his rational mind, liberated from magic and the fear of God. He relies less on his kin than on a range of abstract social systems, such as the State, and on intimate sexual relationships and a few chosen friends.

This is the line pursued by Anthony Giddens in his important works on modernity.[1] In a sense, he presents a stereotype, and historians might argue that such models tend to close our eyes, not open them, when approaching the past. Be that as it may, similar generalizations are common enough amongst historians, many of them closely linked to theories of modernization. One of the problems with a premodern versus modern dichotomy however, as Jean-Claude Schmitt, Aron Gurevich and others have pointed out, is that it reduces the history of individualism to a simple evolutionary process. Once you have pinpointed the moment when the modern individual consciousness begins, you only have to follow its steady rise. The result is a very crude picture of premodernity and the individual.[2] In reality, as Georg Misch emphasized some sixty years ago in his classic work, *Geschichte der Autobiographie*, long before nineteenth-century liberalism and psychoanalysis there were periods when self-knowledge and self-observation flourished in Europe.[3] The Renaissance in fourteenth- and fifteenth-century Italy is often mentioned as an age when individuality developed, as is the Enlightenment in the eighteenth century.

Yet turn to Augustine back in the fourth century, and in his *Confessions* you will find a splendid example of profound self-reflection; and the twelfth and thirteenth centuries have been called a first Renaissance, one that led to greater individual consciousness. In monasteries and churches in the Middle Ages, people discovered that their human nature—*ego, anima, se ip-sum*—was something shared by all human beings—an *imago Dei*. In fact, throughout the Middle Ages there were thinkers who took an interest in the inner human landscape, and contributed to what in earlier research was called the development of the individual, and what more recently has been termed subject-formation.

Clearly, though, mediaeval man did not invent individualism in our sense of autonomy. Neither did mediaeval man indulge in the exhibition of selfhood without severe restrictions. He was constantly aware of his place in the community of honorable men; of the requirements of group norms, and how they commanded the respect of others. Aron Gurevich provides a winning analysis of this complex blend of individualism and collectivism in the mediaeval mind. He views the emergence of individual consciousness as a series of waves travelling through the Middle Ages, and he emphasizes the importance of anchoring our understanding firmly in the social context of the day. For example, the Church and Christian faith alike demanded that all individuals examine their conscience, looking for sins of omission and commission, and for the virtues that would enable them to live a Christian life. Add to this the fact that across much of Northern Europe the vast majority of the population lived in solitary farms and had individual responsibility for their households and their lands,[4] and we must acknowledge that it is simplistic to regard premodern man as the embodiment of collectivism and modern man as the prototype of individuality. The combinations are much more subtle.

What elements, then, are involved in the confirming of a sense of individualism? Paul Ricoeur describes the "hermeneutics of the self" as "the dialectic of selfhood (*ipse*) and sameness (*idem*), and finally the dialectic of selfhood and otherness." He refers to *ipse*, selfhood, as something that only becomes visible in relation to others. *Idem*, sameness, is quite different, for it refers to consistency and permanence in time, the quality of being the same unique person again and again. Both *ipse* and *idem* are integral to the development of the individual, but while *ipse*—the active self revealed here and now—is compatible with the idea of an individual having a variable and unstable identity, *idem*—the consistent self over time—is difficult to reconcile with such postmodern notions. Ricoeur tries to solve this by referring to narratology, arguing that it is in the *emplotment* of our life story that identity is constructed and the dialectic of *ipse* and *idem* is resolved.[5] He furthermore acknowledges

97

the potential of an intertwined relationship between autobiographical narration—the construction of the self—and the idea of a friend as both separate from the self and conjoined with it.

Writing an autobiography is not a matter of including everything that has ever happened to you; on the contrary, it requires a strict selection of facts, the creation of a plot or story, perhaps even identifying the great turning points in your life. You cannot write everything, you have to choose. What is constructed in an autobiography, in the Italian philosopher Adriana Cavarero's word, is "the narratable self."[6] In the worst instances, autobiographies degenerate into naive egocentrism, but equally, autobiography can mean a scrutiny of the self in a social context. After all, the author does not live in a vacuum, but is conscious that he or she is formed in social interplay. Thus, autobiographies may emphasize the friendships that the author thinks are important for his or her own life.

However, there are different kinds of autobiography. One might even talk of different sub-genres, from the political autobiography in which the author tries to defend his mistakes and glorify his successes, to the intellectual biography, prompted by some learned society or scholarly academy. Autobiographical passages may also be hidden in a book that is not otherwise constructed as a narrative of the author's life and texts. Such is the case with Montaigne, to whom I will return below.

For my purpose here, I have chosen a few autobiographical or semi-autobiographical works to discuss how their authors depict the writing-subject's friends and the nature of friendship. The texts have enduring literary and intellectual worth. They are from very different ages, and of very different character. For the sake of simplicity I initially term them *existential autobiography* (exemplified by Augustine of Hippo and Petrarch), *intellectual autobiography* (Michel de Montaigne and Giambattista Vico), and *emotional autobiography* (Jean-Jacques Rousseau). By "existential" I refer to the author's awareness of his vulnerable situation as a human being: he is mortal; he wishes to be happy and do good, but he will also face serious challenges. It goes without saying that these terms serve only as an initial, crude classification, with no ambition to reproduce the full complexity of these remarkable texts. Montaigne's, for example, is not an autobiography at all in one sense, but his *Essays* do have autobiographical components. And his disquisitions are certainly both intellectual, existential, and emotional. Augustine's is a prime example of an existential autobiography; yet it also includes remarkable intellectual observations.

All autobiographers create their selves in their stories about themselves. But they also talk about friends.

To understand yourself through a friend

Before we turn to these autobiographies there is good reason to return to Aristotle (384–322 BC) and his *Nichomachean Ethics*. The *Ethics* was not only the inspiration of much later thought on the nature and function of friendship; it was also about the virtues that good people should possess, and the process they should undergo in attaining self-knowledge, wisdom, and happiness. In practice this means that the discussions of individual development and friendship are intermingled, and that Aristotle contends that self-knowledge is increased by social intercourse with good friends.

Our actions, Aristotle writes, have but one objective. Their ultimate goal is that excellent state we choose to call happiness. The individual seeks personal happiness, but it is even better to seek the common good, happiness for society as a whole.

For although the good of an individual is identical with the good of a state, yet the good of the state, whether in attainment or in preservation, is evidently greater and more perfect. For while in an individual by himself it is something to be thankful for, it is nobler and more divine in a nation or state.[7]

Happiness, he continues, subsists in virtue, or in the exercise of excellence or virtue, in thought and action. But how then to attain excellence or virtue, and from what do they emanate? His answer is that virtue is a quality of character by which a balance is struck between extremes. Thus courage stands midway between recklessness and cowardice, generosity between meanness and extravagance, self-possession between brashness and aloofness. Balance, harmony, good judgement; these are Aristotle's touchstones. And character is bound up with prudence (*phronesis*), where prudence should not be confused with the even greater insight, wisdom (*sophia*). Admittedly, *phronesis* is concerned with thought, reflection, and intelligence, but it is also expressed in practical action as statesmanship. *Phronesis* "deals with things as are of human interest and admit of deliberation. For wise deliberation is, as we conceive, the principal function of the prudent man."[8]

For Aristotle, this practical wisdom—the good judgement and ability to take balanced decisions—can be attained through friendship. Perfect friendship is an enterprise between excellent and virtuous individuals. In truth, it is itself a kind of virtue, and is indispensable for all people. Even if you have all imaginable wealth and success, you will still need friends. Friendship in its turn promotes justice and binds society together:

> For friendship is a kind of virtue or implies virtue. It is also indispensable to life. For nobody would choose to live without friends, although he were in possession of every other good. Nay, it seems that if people are rich and hold official and authoritative positions, they have the greatest need of friends; ... for two people have a greater power both of intelligence and of action than either of the two by himself. ... Again, it seems that friendship or love is the bond which holds states together, and that legislators set more store by it than by justice; for concord is apparently akin to friendship, and it is concord that they especially seek to promote.[9]

Here friendship answers for social solidarity, since all forms of solidarity are also social solidarity. It is in this manner that friendship becomes a civic virtue.

Likewise, Aristotle conducts a dialogue with himself about whether a person who has already attained happiness has any need of friends. His conclusion is that it would be unreasonable not to allow the happy man any friends because life weighs heavily on the recluse. Moreover, the individual's ability to develop successful relationships with other people is closely associated with self-knowledge. Friendship proceeds from the individual's relationship to himself, in which the friend is akin to a "second self."[10]

It is thus striking that Aristotle's ideas about how the individual becomes good, virtuous, and happy, are to such an extent entwined with notions of ideal friendship. To my mind, both tend to the common good, and have a bearing on the state of society. It is equally interesting to note Aristotle's message that people must train themselves in self-knowledge, must practice to attain excellence. Intellectual knowledge is something you can be taught, but moral wisdom only comes from experience, he writes. The virtues must therefore be lived out; for example, we only become just through our just actions. It is this that Michel Foucault would later seize on; classical subject-formation was a matter of constant exertions of body and soul, of consciously training one's actions and thoughts with the purpose of becoming an individual who is capable of acting justly. One of several techniques to improve self-examination is the writing of letters or an autobiography.[11]

This leads us straight to some of the great autobiographies of history to see how the authors approach the business of attaining self-knowledge, and the extent to which they do so in the company of their friends.

A sociable man talking to God: Augustine

Augustine of Hippo (AD 354–430) completed his *Confessions* in AD 397. I would venture that he was to mediaeval thought what Weber, Marx, Darwin, and Freud are to modernity's turbulent world of ideas. Even today Augustine's ideas have shown themselves to be remarkably durable as a source of inspiration. His reflections on the elusive concept of time are justly famous; and, it should be noted, influenced Paul Ricoeur.[12] "It is inexact language," writes Augustine, "to speak of three times—past, present, and future. Perhaps it would be exact to say: there are three times, a present of things past, a present of things present, and a present of things to come. In the soul there are these three aspects of time, and I do not see them anywhere else."[13] Indeed, this assertion contains a theory of man's ability to have a historical consciousness and to entertain utopian thought. "For," as he puts it elsewhere, "the mind expects and attends and remembers."[14] *Intentio, attentio,* and *retentio* are thus woven together in human consciousness. We have all the different dimensions of time in our thoughts, simultaneously. Time exists nowhere else. Our ability to combine our conscious memories with our sense of the present and our visions for the future creates not only our individual consciousness, but also our historical consciousness.[15]

Despite the subtlety of these observations, however, Augustine has a sympathetic way of mixing philosophical intellect with an understanding of the vagueness of everyday speech. By all means, let people say that there are three times, the past, the present, and the future, he reasons. It makes no difference as long as we understand what is being said. In the daily confusion of approximations and ambiguities, we can be understood even when we use ill-defined notions.[16] Theoretical models crack and collapse if the terms they are constructed on are imprecise. Humans can cope regardless. Thus Augustine adds tolerance and empathy for the imperfections of everyday life to his intellectual brilliance.

Augustine's autobiography concerns his childhood, youth, and early adulthood, written near the turning point in his life when, after an anguished inner struggle, he converted to Christianity. The settings are the town of Tagaste in present-day Algeria, his birthplace; Carthage, then a seat of learning; Rome and Milan, the places where he taught rhetoric; the port of Ostia, where his beloved mother Monica died; and finally North Africa again. The autobiography covers the thirty-odd years from his birth to his return as a Christian convert to North Africa, where ultimately he would become Bishop of Hippo Regius.

In his *Confessions*, Augustine conducts a dialogue with God. The account of his childhood and youth serves to build up the tension before the story's decisive moment—Augustine's capitulation to Christianity. The thread that runs through the *Confessions* is the sinful man's path to salvation. After a rather wild youth, Augustine acknowledges his misery, and begins to ponder the meaning of life, but for a long time he finds no answers even though he becomes an eager scholar. He hears of God and Christianity but cannot at first accept the Christian faith. Finally, exhausted by his doubts, his sorrow and agony, he abandons all resistance and collapses before God, in complete despair. After that, his life found meaning, he tells us.[17]

The historian Peter Brown has pointed out that Augustine's inner contemplation links the *Confessions* to the classical tradition of religious philosophy. But its emotional tone gives it a "modern" appearance. Augustine is clear about what is important to him, and he expresses it as the story of his heart and his emotions. Similarly, what we would call intellectual shifts register in him as emotions. Augustine does not say "it changed my view," but "it changed the way I felt"—*mutavit affectum meum*.[18] He places great weight on intuition, the unconscious, and dreams.[19] In the midst of this existential narrative there is still time for other, smaller stories. A number of them are about friends and friendship.

The image Augustine gives of himself as a very little boy is vivid and far from idyllic. He likes to play, is disobedient towards his teachers, and likes to compete with his classmates.[20] It is not an altogether positive picture. He even goes so far as to try to win games by cheating. But the boy is quick; he has a good memory; he is skilled with words; and he finds joy in friendship.[21] Naturally, in talking about his bad side Augustine is employing a well-worn narrative technique; the worse now, the sharper the contrast will be when he later converts to Christianity. Nevertheless, the details of his childhood adventures are most probably not mere fiction. Rather, they represent an effort to relate some, although not all, significant memories about his development that have stayed in his consciousness.

Friends, in Augustine's account of his childhood, can be both a good thing and a bad thing, depending on what instinct they appeal to. The problem is underscored in the account of Augustine's youth. Here the author positively revels in his own depravity; the wickedness drawn out of him by friends who are even more sophisticated in their vices.[22] He writes of his expedition with other "young scoundrels" to steal pears just for the fun of it. It is in the wake of this episode that we find the first, general reflection on friendship as an evil temptation.[23] Augustine spells out the dangers of camaraderie. Left to his own devices, he writes, he would not have stolen a single pear:

> Alone I would not have committed that crime, in which my pleasure lay not in what I was stealing but in the act of theft. But had I been alone, it would

have given me absolutely no pleasure, nor would I have committed it. Friendship can be a dangerous enemy, a seduction of the mind lying beyond the reach of investigation.[24]

It is this largely evil brand of friendship that haunts Augustine for a while yet.

As a youth he travels to Carthage to study. But it was lust that was to absorb his thoughts and actions.[25] However, it is when Augustine is in his twenties and has begun to teach rhetoric, that he undergoes a serious change of heart. He is struck by grief when a friend dies.[26] The grief is so strong that Augustine is gripped by a loathing of life and a fear of death. What finally enables him to recover is the comfort of finding new friends. With great insight, he contemplates the power and delight of this friendship between mature men:

There were other things which occupied my mind in the company of my friends: to make conversation, to share a joke, to perform mutual acts of kindness, to read together well-written books, to share in trifling and serious matters, to disagree though without animosity—just as a person debates within himself—and in the very rarity of disagreement to find the salt of normal harmony, to teach each other something or to learn from one another, to long with impatience for those absent, to welcome them with gladness on their arrival. These and other signs come from the heart ...acting as fuel to set our minds on fire and out of many to forge unity.[27]

Indeed, the adult Augustine does not lack for friends. They play a critical role in the *Confessions*, and he reflects time and again on his friendships at different stages of life. There are two whom we can count as his intimates: Alypius and Nebridius. Alypius came from the same town as Augustine, and had once been his pupil. In Rome, Augustine bumps into Alypius, who is now a lawyer, and they become close friends. Nebridius had also left his home near Carthage and "in his burning enthusiasm for the truth and for wisdom" had gone to Italy to live with Augustine.[28] Alypius and Nebridius are thus bound to him in the religious process that leads up to the conversion, and were members of the small group who made up a spiritual fellowship centred on Augustine.

When the reader of the *Confessions* finally arrives at the description of Augustine's conversion, an account of his torments of insecurity and existential agony paves the way. One day, when Augustine is at home with Alypius, they are visited by their fellow countryman from Africa. He catches sight of a book that turns out to be by St Paul, and begins to tell them about the monks and the miracles of the Church. Augustine is deeply affected, "distressed not only in mind but in appearance."[29] Together he and Alypius go out into the garden, where Augustine becomes so distressed that he moves away from his friend's side, and collapses in tears under a fig tree. Through his tears, he suddenly hears a child in a nearby house chanting the phrase, "Pick up and read, pick up and read." He is certain it is a divine command, and hurries to tell Alypius, who is equally overcome by emotion. And so they abandon all their doubts and resistance, and give in to the miracle of finding God.

Thus in his *Confessions*, Augustine writes in different ways about his friends in various phases of his life, using a clear moral hierarchy in the evaluation of the relationships. In his view there are friends who bring joy, the very embodiment of pleasant reciprocity, and there are friends who "lead us into temptation." Yet most of all there is a form of friendship that according to Augustine is only good; the ideal friendship that stretches out beyond the pleasures of private life, to God.

In his autobiography Augustine is far from being pictured as a recluse: he is a man who thrives amongst people; a faithful friend and charming company. This observation is also made by Peter Brown in his fine biography. In the *Confessions* we meet an expansive social being, a man who always wants to have his friends about him. Autobiography may well be a form of self-therapy, and Augustine is absorbed in his own soul and his own emotions, but despite this, he is almost never alone, and "rarely do we find him thinking in solitude."[30]

Yet while he is plainly a sociable and pleasant man, alive to the wishes of his companions, Augustine throughout his *Confessions* embodies the selfhood—*ipse*—of individuality: he may be close to his friends, teachers, and pupils; he may be influenced by them; but nevertheless he is different from all of them. He is a unique person, and well aware of his uniqueness. On the other hand, it seems to me that his narrative clearly recognizes the sameness of his individuality—the *idem* quality of his character, expressed as permanence and coherence—only when he has converted and is a true Christian. After that he has become the person he wants to identify with fully, for the rest of his life.

Augustine is also a philosopher of history and systemizer of philosophical ideas. When writing of friendship in a broad sense, above all in the nineteenth book of *De civitate Dei*, he sets it firmly in the context of the Greek philosophers. Here Augustine discusses what distinguishes a life well lived. He concludes that "this happy life is social, and for its own sake values the good of friends as its own, just as it wishes for them, for their own sake, what it wishes for itself."[31] We can glimpse here Aristotle's ideas of friendship, albeit through a Christian glass. The happy life must be social, since how else could God's city have been attained if the saints' lives had not also been social?[32] Yet Augustine does not commend this ideal without qualification, since a Christian also must live privately with God. Therefore he reminds us of the insults, the envy, the conflicts and wars that are just as much a part of our social existence.[33]

When it comes to the more precise remarks about friendship, Augustine is very close to the classical authorities, as Marie Aquinas McNamara has pointed out. What is new in Augustine's approach is the idea that God is the fount and origin of friendship; that friendship must be anchored in God; and that Christian friendship transcends human limitations and is rooted in divine grace and charity. Only in heaven does friendship first reach perfection.[34]

In sum, Augustine appears in his *Confessions* as a sensitive man, armed with a sharp intellect and social ease. He is outgoing and has many friends, yet at the same time inner foreboding drives him. He conducts an uninterrupted dialogue with God. He speaks often of his friends. They are important to him, for better or worse. Friendship can lead a man astray, that much he recognizes. But he is also certain that friendship can give support and comfort; knowledge and joy; company on the path to righteousness. The best friends are the ones who will share with him the experience of becoming Christian. Thus far Augustine's thoughts on friendship are rooted in classical doctrines of reciprocity, trust, and free choice. But where Aristotle rated an ideal friendship based on wisdom and good character that could serve the public good, Augustine looks for a true friendship in the service of God. The Christianization of the classical philosophy of friendship began with Augustine.

A dialogue with Augustine: Petrarch

A thousand years later, Petrarch spoke directly to Augustine. This despite the fact that he is more associated with the Renaissance, and its condescending views on mediaeval thought, than with Christian reflection.

Francesco Petrarca, or Petrarch (1307–1374) is most famous for his poems to Laura, yet he also left a series of diary entries which amount to a kind of fragmented autobiography. Initially they were secret, but they are thought to have been written and revised in the 1340s and 1350s. In them, he conducts what amounts to a self-tormenting dialogue with Augustine, who takes the role of the super-ego. Together they explore "Francesco's" weaknesses. The fictitious Augustine drives "Francesco" ever further in confessing the truth about himself; and uncomfortable truths they are too, overflowing with vanity, avarice, ambition, and lust.

Petrarch is ambivalent towards friends and friendship. You cannot possibly be completely frank with your friends, he announces; even if you were to confide in them, however real your tears, you would soon return quickly to "the normal order." It is as if something holds you back from complete sincerity when you are with friends, he says. There are also limits to what he is ready to do for his friends:

> I am not so low and heartless that I do not care for my friends, especially those whose goodness and worth win me over. There are indeed people I admire, venerate, love, or even pity. But at the same

time I am not so generous as to ruin myself for them.[35]

Friendship definitely has its limits for Petrarch. It also has degrees. Some friends inspire respect and love, others compassion. It is clear that, in this, Petrarch differs considerably from the classical ideal of friendship. In his version, friendship is not a bond between people who are equal; there is a hierarchy in the relationship. True, friendship comprises mutual exchange, but not without limitations. By and large we can interpret Petrarch's view of friendship as being free of illusion, even a touch cynical. Not for him depravity for his friends' sakes. He believes that even amongst friends, openheartedness has its limits, since no friendship will survive the ugliness of a heated argument. It is impossible even in a close friendship to plumb the existential depths of decay, death, and the futility of life.

Petrarch reflects less on the general idea of friendship than on his actual friends, yet woven into the account of how he has treated them, we can still catch sight of his notion of an ideal friendship. It embodies love and respect. It does not inspire unease and hostility, but rather joy and the willing exchange of ideas. And it is not easy to find.

Petrarch lived in an age when the discourse on the autonomy of the individual had come a step nearer our own than in Augustine's time. Certainly, Petrarch moves in what is still a religious world, but he is at pains to shield his integrity and his inner life both in relation to his friends and in relation to God. A friend is to Petrarch not a second self, a helpmate in excellence in public life, as Aristotle imagined the ideal friend. Neither is he like a brother in the existential search for God, as in Augustine's *Confessions*. A true friend for Petrarch is a person with whom you can talk about serious matters, but Petrarch finds such friendships quite rare. It seems, paradoxically, that he has no faith in one of the most fundamental aspects of friendship—trust. In that respect, he also tends to underestimate the potential which friends have to help each other in the process of self-examination, in subject-formation. If friends flinch from speaking openly about their fears and resentments, how can friendship help the individual to know himself better?

The need for loneliness: Montaigne

The philosopher and writer Michel de Montaigne (1533–1592) has been credited with bringing something new to self-reflection, as well as changing views on friendship. This makes him interesting in the present context. His *Essays* may not be an autobiography in the true sense, for they are not intended to provide a chronological account of his personal development, but they do amount to a fluent, sometimes repetitive exposition of what he has read and thought and seen. They also have a specific biographical background that goes some way to explaining why Montaigne is so fixated on friendship in the *Essays*.[36]

For Montaigne, friendship above all served as the individual's refuge from society, a private place to search your soul and discover the scope of your mind together with a good friend. Montaigne thus marks a transition in the intellectual history of friendship. As we have seen, the great classical and mediaeval minds generally held that an ideal friendship aspired to do good for a higher end: for Aristotle, by associating with the best of friends to become as wise and just a man in civic life as in private; for Augustine and Bernard of Clairvaux, by joining with a friend to seek God. In modern society, the emphasis is instead on friendship as private, personal, and emotional. Montaigne falls somewhere between the two.[37]

In his *Essays* of 1580, Montaigne gives a whole

chapter to the subject of friendship. Here we will find a careful attempt to distil what is special about friendship when compared with other forms of close relationship. Montaigne writes of a consummate friendship between two people of the same sex, of amity of a deep and heartfelt kind. This relationship is quite distinct from other close relations between the same sex, be they paternal or fraternal. Friendship subsists in an exchange between equals; this cannot be the case between father and son, who are too unalike. A father cannot share all his thoughts with his son "lest an improper familiarity should be created." Equally, a son cannot come to his father with the same truths that he can share with a friend. It is not proper, writes Montaigne. The relationship between brothers admittedly resembles that between friends, but the fact that brothers will share their father's inheritance often leads to conflict: "the complication of interest, the division of estates, the probability of pursuing the same profession for their advancement in life, greatly slacken the fraternal tie." Likewise, Montaigne considers love between men and women to be more intense than friendship, but at the same time more fleeting. Friendship in its ideal form has very different qualities:

Friendship subsists in mutual exchange, in which both can speak the truth.

Friendship is "a steady flame" of all-embracing warmth and kindness, but equally it is free from the extremes of passion.

Friendship has "no other idea than that of itself."

Friends wish each other well.

Perfect friendship is indissoluble.

Friendship both sustains and heartens ("… had I such a friend to attract and encourage me, as I once possessed."[38]

What we see here is an idealization of friendship. To be honest, writes Montaigne, true friendship requires such unanimity and fortitude that he doubts that women are sufficient to the task. He thus cannot envisage ideal friendship other than between men. In this he was not only treading classical, patriarchal ground, but also the equally firm ground of early-modern gender hierarchies.

In many respects, classical ideas underpin Montaigne's reflections. Cicero had said we can best recognize a friend by looking in the mirror.[39] Montaigne writes of a fusion of two selves, of one self in two bodies:

But the attachment to which I allude has no other idea than that of itself, and is so interwoven into one piece, that there is no appearance of the seam by which the component parts were first united. If I should be importuned to give the reason for my regard, I can no otherwise express myself than because it was he, because it was I.[40]

In the ideal friendship, it is because of this fusion that we can dare wearing our hearts on our sleeves. Yet Montaigne also admits that in our daily lives we have more acquaintances than close friends, more of the "common" or conventional friendships that do not demand exclusivity. Occasionally they come about almost by accident.[41] However, none of these relationships comes close to the profound, sublime symbiosis that the ideal friendship means for Montaigne. Here we can glimpse Aristotle's calibration of the different forms of friendship: there are those entered into for personal advantage or for pleasure, but the most important is the ideal friendship between virtuous equals.

Montaigne's preoccupation with friendship in the *Essays* has its biographical reasons. He sorely missed his friend Étienne de La Boétie, who had died in 1563, and who had been a kindred soul and dialogue partner. But we know very little about this friendship. Some historians believe that to some extent it should be seen as an *ex post facto* rationalization, principally intended to legitimize the otherwise unfocussed, rather egocentric style that Montaigne was the first to establish as the essayist's.[42] The long-departed friend is constructed at the same time as Montaigne fashions himself as an author and philosopher of friendship.

It is interesting that Montaigne also praises solitude elsewhere in his *Essays*. Solitude can save us from dangerous "crowd behavior": ambition, avarice, indecision, fear, and lust. Solitude exists so that we can reclaim ourselves. However, it is not something that can be achieved simply by avoiding other people. You have to create your own space within yourself, a place where you are free, where the duties of friendship are turned inwards on yourself:

> When once worldly affairs have taken strong possession of our minds, they will follow us into cloisters or deserts; and if a man does not first disengage himself from inordinate desires, and relieve his mind from the burden with which he is oppressed, he will receive more harm than good by removing from place to place. ... We then in vain seek

that true repose from solitude, which may be possessed even in populous cities and the courts of kings, with a right disposition, though I confess more commodiously when separated from them. ... We must reserve a back shop, a withdrawing room, wholly to ourselves, where we may find true liberty.[43]

Again, this yearning to withdraw from the world had a specific motive in Montaigne's case. After fifteen years as a lawyer in Bordeaux he quit office in 1571, only 38 years old. He wanted to spend his time in thought, to be alone on his estate. He retired to the tower of the Château de Montaigne, to his inner space. What was original about his project was not his retirement as such. Several ancient Romans had enjoyed their *otium* in their country retreats. Mediaeval mystics had turned to introspection as a means to knowledge, and withdrew from the world. But the religious soul-searching they had in mind was aimed at *escaping* themselves; to reach God. Montaigne, on the other hand, wanted to *escape into* himself by writing.[44]

Thus in Montaigne we find a line drawn between the outer world, which he often criticized, and the inner world of human soul which we must reach by living quite alone. Ideal friendship impinges on that inner world. It is not fame, but rather reciprocal goodness that people need in their inner worlds.

The exact purpose of such good friendship is not entirely clear in Montaigne, however. There are clear references to Aristotle in his belief that friendship is conducive to justice and civic life. Yet in Montaigne's version of friendship, it is solely a way for us to attain self-knowledge. Ideal friendship, he seems to say, is a means in itself, existing only so that two close friends can get to know themselves better. If that is true, Montaigne's writings on friendship have less to do with making friendship personal and exclusive (as opposed to public and inclusive), and more to do with seeing friendship as a tool for a growing individual consciousness.[45] That it is a desire for self-knowledge that drives Montaigne is evident:

> I have simply devoted my time to the advantage of my relations and friends, ... I am desirous to appear simple and unadorned, without study or artifice. As it is myself whom I mean to represent.[46]

It is interesting that Montaigne, in discussing his views on the individual, does not attempt to argue that human nature is coherent and unchanging. In this respect he appears quite modern, postmodern even, in his acceptance that individuals can be contradictory and inconsistent. Montaigne goes so far as to express surprise that authors try to rationalize the people they write about; that they try to find a logic for their actions and opinions. People are often irresolute, he writes, and therefore they are rarely intrinsically coherent or stable. Therefore he finds it strange that writers persist in trying to create a consistent whole out of their changeable human material:

> I am surprised when men attempt to define characters; especially as irresolution appears to be the fault of our nature ... but considering the natural instability of our opinions, the best authors may be sometimes mistaken.[47]

It would seem that in writing in the *Essays* about the development of the individual and the significance of friendship, Montaigne allows himself to adopt different standpoints that are not always easy to reconcile. On the one hand, he writes about an ideal friendship that to all intents and purposes is a symbiotic relationship between two good men. On the other hand, he seems quite critical of the "ordinary" friendships that do not have this quality of unique duality, and he underlines the importance of withdrawing completely from the company of others, of seeking out a private space, in order to attain self-knowledge. It is only here that we can "reclaim" ourselves. But at the same time he realizes that for most of us, "ourselves" is neither a consistent or permanent identity. The unpredictability of human nature prevents it.

The autobiography of an intellectual: Vico

If we move on to the seventeenth century, we find Giambattista Vico (1668–1744) and a prime example of one of the autobiographical sub-genres which became more common in the eighteenth century: the intellectual autobiography. Vico was a leading philosopher of his day and he has also later attracted scholarly interest because of his view of history moving in cycles. In later life, he was urged by a learned society to write his autobiography, and the resultant work amounts to a personal history of science. It followed the professor's incremental deepening of his theses and his working practices, and his ever-widening sources of inspiration. He took a couple of years to write it at the end of the 1720s, and published it in Naples in December 1730.[48]

His autobiography conveys an image of a scientist

who seeks knowledge with consuming energy. He has an enormous appetite for books, and rattles through everything from poetry to legal tracts. Homer or Tacitus, Plato or Bacon—he devours and digests it all. He launches his own theses with rigor and rhetorical brilliance. He was a professor at a time when there was more honor than money in academe, and those who wrote for a living had to eke out their existence with gifts and annuities. He wanted to write, he wanted to become famous for his ideas; he could not afford to be disrespectful to cardinals, princes, and their ilk, and he was happy to make a show of his recognition thus far. This was the heyday of the patron–client relationship.[49]

What we see in Vico's autobiography is how a giant of learning constructs an intellectual self-image, addressed to a circle of peers. It is from this perspective that he chooses to single out certain friends, all without exception his equal in talent. They are friends in discourse, and they share an enthusiasm for clever ideas. They form an intellectual network.[50] He speaks with particular warmth of the philosopher and scientist, Paolo Doria, and of Domenico d'Ausilio, whom Vico esteems because he had spoken approvingly of some of Vico's work, although normally he was very critical. So what Vico constructs in his autobiography is neither a story of friends, a philosophy of friendship, nor a narrative of intense self-reflection. Rather, it is a description of intellectual work and intellectual influences, in a time that showed enthusiasm for scholarly work and new scientific ideas, but still offered few safe professional positions for scholars. He had to trust the support of patrons.

In one particular passage in his autobiography, children and friends are said to have been very much in evidence when Vico was preparing a lecture, "as was their wont." It is the only hint at a life that amounted to more than intellectual exchange; a life punctuated by kitchen bustle, children in full cry, the general hum of everyday existence. Yet on the whole it is probably in the nature of this kind of intellectual autobiography that friendship will be equated with scholarly dialogue, its very existence based on praise and respectful debate between intellectual equals. To adopt much more recent terminology, it could be said that Vico's autobiography displays his friends as a thought collective, as an intellectual network.[51]

Love before friendship: Rousseau

Let us then turn to Rousseau. He lived at a time that, according to many scholars, not only saw the origins of unfettered modern individualism, but also a sentimental cult of friendship fostered in letters and epistolary novels.[52]

When Jean-Jacques Rousseau (1712–1778) began to write his autobiography, he was in his fifties. His memoirs would not be published until the 1780s, after his death, when they appeared as *Les Confessions*. Their scope is magnificent. Yes, one might argue even grandiose and self-indulgent, but for all that, characteristic of the age. Not for him Augustine's opening words about a dialogue with God, reflecting on the search for inner knowledge, neither Montaigne's more humble declaration of his wish to show the truth about himself as a simple man. Rousseau wants to tell the unvarnished truth, and places himself firmly centre stage for all to behold; a unique person in the world:

> I am resolved on an undertaking that has no model and will have no imitator. I want to show my fellow men a man in all the truth of nature; and this man is to be myself.
>
> Myself alone. I feel in my heart and I know men. I am not made like any that I have seen; I venture to believe that I was not made like any that exist. If I am not more deserving, at least I am different. ...

I have shown myself as I was, contemptible and vile when that is how I was, good, generous, sublime, when that is how I was.[53]

Rousseau remembers the shame of the stupid things he has done, but also the heightened sense of life that love brings. He conjures up erotic temptation, envy, jealousy, ennui, and the happiness of total absorption in the fictitious people and places of a novel. Early on he provides the key to understanding the young Rousseau, or at least to the understanding he wishes us to have. In the book's first pages, we find an account of a boy who takes rapidly and enthusiastically to reading, who devours novels. He approaches the world and its creatures using his intuition and emotions rather than cognition: "I had conceived nothing; I had felt the whole."[54] It is interesting here to compare with Augustine. Augustine, as I have mentioned, did not say that something changed his view. Instead he talked in terms of a cognitive process involving emotions: *mutavit affectum meum*—it affected the way I felt.

The overriding feeling that runs through the passages on his childhood and youth is a love of women who show the young Rousseau kindness and motherly concern. Since in the eighteenth century talk of love was often dressed in the language of friendship, such relationships could also be depicted as bonds between friends.

If love of women is at the heart of Rousseau's *Confessions*, friendship with other boys and men still plays an important role in his story. Three friends stand out in his narrative about his youth: his cousin Bernard and his companions Bâcle and Venture. He and Bernard work and play together; they are inseparable, and their characters agree well. When they do quarrel, it is never for long, and they derive such joy from being together that they do not need anyone else. It is a friendship that, like love, is characterized by closeness and exclusivity.[55] His friendship with Bernard never becomes problematic, but it does fade, without bitterness, as Rousseau grows older, and the social gap between him and Bernard, a gentleman's son, becomes increasingly marked.

Brief but intense friendship is what Jean-Jacques later experiences with a travelling companion, Bâcle. Their friendship lasts about six weeks, and their final separation is not a cause of concern to either. The friendship in this case evidently sprang from finding good company on a long journey. It was a relationship distinguished by mutual happiness under special circumstances. But it was to be short-lived.[56] Rousseau's youthful adventures also lead him into an acquaintance with Venture de Villeneuve, who is depicted as a gifted rake. Jean-Jacques describes his feelings towards this friend in terms of enthusiasm and delight. For a time he is quite simply enchanted. But again, his feelings fade in due course.[57]

Gradually, as he puts it himself, Rousseau approaches the phase when his past intersects with his present existence. He is now an adult, and the direction his interests will take him is becoming clearer. Many of the friendships he makes in this period will last, and he holds them dear. Yet he is always concerned that his friends are drawn to him only because he has become famous, and he is struck by nostalgia for:

> ... that happy obscurity, when those who said they were my friends were so, and loved me for myself alone, out of simple goodness of heart and not out of vanity at being connected with a famous man or out of a secret desire to discover new ways of harming him.[58]

Amongst the old friends of his youth that Rousseau encounters at the start of his career is Monsieur de Gauffecourt, "one of the most amiable men that has ever existed."[59] He is described in the first part of the

Confessions as generally well liked, straightforward, and honorable. He successfully manages his affairs and unselfishly tries to help all his friends. Rousseau's only reservation is that de Gauffecourt "served his friends with zeal, or rather he made friends with people whom he could help, and was adroit at seeing to his own interests while vigorously pursuing theirs."[60] De Gauffecourt's almost indiscriminate friendship seems to catch Rousseau off balance. It seems that he would prefer to feel more exclusive, more uniquely singled out by his friends.

For Rousseau, as for so many before him, there are degrees of friendship. Happy camaraderie or a delight taken in a charming person stands in contrast to steady friendships that endure over many years. He characterizes his friends as loyal, sincere, and inseparable—and generally his equals. They share joy and fellow feeling. In his descriptions of actual friendships, we glimpse his ideal of friendship. For Rousseau, the perfect friendship does not mean Aristotelian virtue and wisdom in the service of the greater good; nor is its ultimate goal a union with God, as it was for Augustine. No, for Rousseau, friendship remains firmly in the personal sphere, and its kernel is psychology and emotion. His best friends love him for his own sake, not for his great works or his fame as a writer; friendship's essence is reciprocal goodness and goodwill, and by all means let it be a mite exclusive.

Rousseau liked to think of himself as unique. That he was. Today we can also see that his reflections on friendship nevertheless mirror his times. In eighteenth-century France, old political structures were questioned; new public debating spaces emerged; the arts saw the cultivation of the individual and the private; literacy increased, and people read like never before.[61] The boundaries between private and public were renegotiated. Emotions were discussed and defined. And in the middle of this ferment we find Rousseau, a man who does not discuss friendship as a philosophy or an ideal, but speaks of his friends from a psychological and emotional viewpoint in a narrative that focuses on the uniqueness of his ego, on subject-formation. To this extent, he was very much a child of his time.

Individuality and sociability

Friendship and friends are rarely the principal themes in the autobiographical narratives I have studied; unsurprisingly, given an autobiography's focus is almost always the author himself, and its subject his struggle to develop his personality.[62] That said, in all the texts I have analyzed, self-improvement and the acquisition of self-knowledge is always dependent on the individual's relationship to *something else*—an idea, an ambition, a wish to achieve something important. For Augustine, it was a relationship with God; for Petrarch, an existential fear of death; for Vico, a passion for intellectual development. Montaigne is more difficult to pinpoint, but it is evident that in his eagerness to understand himself better, he was spurred on in an emotional as well as an intellectual process. Love drives Rousseau. However, the process of subject-formation is as a rule also a matter of the individual having relationships with *someone else*. The more exhaustive texts in particular—Augustine, Montaigne and Rousseau—contain many observations on friendship that are worth considering. The authors acknowledge their debt of gratitude to close friends, and Augustine's and Rousseau's narratives include several stories about their friends. Self-reflection, in other words, by no means precludes generosity to others. It is implicitly recognized that individuality is developed in dialogue with friends.

In fact, the Italian philosopher Adriana Cavarero is probably right when she says that autobiography does not really make the subject–ego any the more self-absorbed. On the contrary, the ego exposes its life history to the gaze of others who are necessary as fellow actors or potential readers. It is therefore unfair to speak of such narratives as narcissism, she argues. By recounting their lives, by revealing their true selves, the narrators lay themselves bare. The internal becomes external.[63] In the process, the narrator is also made visible as a social being.

Some of the authors are aware of their predecessors; indeed, they conduct a dialogue with other autobiographers. Petrarch spoke directly to Augustine in a series of fictive conversations. Montaigne was familiar with both the classical philosophy of friendship and Augustine. Rousseau was obviously familiar with Augustine, and the significance of calling his account *Les Confessions* is not lost on us. No doubt he was au fait with Montaigne as well. But Rousseau belonged to a later age, and had a different purpose. Unlike Augustine, he did not converse with God, but wanted to show the unvarnished reality of a more modern individual. It is interesting to note that Rousseau and Augustine are similar in talking of the processes of self-knowledge in terms of emotion rather than cognition. Both men register a fresh insight as something that changes the way they felt, not the way they thought. In contrast, Rousseau resembles Montaigne in his avowed intent to use his autobiography to describe himself precisely as he is, although he is less humble than Montaigne in his approach.

It is significant that none of these writers name many close friends. All draw a distinction between passing acquaintances and brief companionships on the one hand, and really significant friends on the other. Reciprocal delight, trust, and concern are assumed by all to be the ingredients of a good friendship. Petrarch seems to be the most pessimistic about the possibility to finding complete trust in a friendship.

Augustine is the most instructive when it comes to dangerous friendship, the kind that will most certainly lead us into temptation. Petrarch is particularly doubtful whether a friendship can survive if the friend is subjected to severe criticism. Nor is he certain that his friends are able or willing to join him in plumbing the existential depths of his soul and his fears of death. Vico, on the other hand, is serenely confident that intellectuals can criticize each other in the heat of debate without jeopardizing their friendships.

Another observation is that the friends held up for our admiration by these male writers are, as a rule, men. It seems it was natural for these five authors, just like the classical philosophers of friendship, to describe their friendships with other men—younger, older, or of the same age. Montaigne even expressed serious doubts as to whether women could ever achieve the depth and warmth of ideal friendship. All five lived at times when men's legitimate relationships with women remained firmly framed within a family context. Augustine, Petrarch, Montaigne, Vico and Rousseau belonged to an old world, a premodern world, in which women did not move with the same sense of entitlement as men, be it in religious, scholarly, or artistic circles.

Finally, to what extent did friends help these authors develop their individuality, to form the subject? And does the process of subject-formation refer to the demonstration of selfhood in relation to others, or the proof of the sameness of the author's character? How do these men handle what Ricoeur calls the dialectic of *ipse* and *idem* in writing their identity and constructing the plot of their life? Here, Augustine's and Rousseau's extensive writings are particularly interesting to compare, for in my view, they actually display striking similarities on this point. In the stories of their childhood and early friends, their identities are revealed mainly in the quality of selfhood:

here am I, with my friends, looking for joy and pleasure; I was different from other people, but still not a grown man of solid character. In both autobiographies, however, there comes a defining moment. For Augustine, it is his conversion to Christianity; for Rousseau, his love for a woman. After this turning point, it is my view that they both construct identities that they are willing to recognize as mature personalities, identities that embody not only selfhood (*ipse*) but also permanence of character and coherence over time (*idem*). Thus they both undergo a cognitive process and acquire self-knowledge, but they do so with a combination of intellectual reflection and strong emotion. And in both phases of their lives, before and after their turning points, a select few friends are party to the process. If God is the great Other for Augustine, and Woman and Sexual Love the great Others for Rousseau, friends perform the necessary role of "other Other" for them both.

Between Augustine and Rousseau we find Montaigne, articulating thoughts about human nature that today seem remarkably modern, even postmodern. In his *Essays* there is no attempt to construct a narrative of authorial self as a chronological, coherent story; you will search in vain for a defining moment. However, in writing about himself and his friends, Montaigne refers back to his long-gone ideal friend. Having lost this very special friend, Montaigne's only recourse in his search for self-knowledge is solitude. But for Montaigne, the needs of subject-formation do not seem to require coherence or permanence of self—*idem*. This is a quality rarely achieved in the attitudes and actions of individuals, he claims, and it is futile for authors try to construct consistent characters out of complex and mutable human beings.

The genre of the ego has, in other words, not given birth to pure narcissism, but rather to a complex and inclusive series of reflections on the self and the other, and on the self and the meaning of life. Man is a self-interpreting animal, but also a social animal. In different ways, all the autobiographies that I have examined demonstrate that narratives of the self are intertwined with stories of friends and friendship. "Me and my friends" has proved to be an interesting and rewarding topic. It shows not only that the gaining of self-knowledge in dialogue with others is probably a universal, trans-historical phenomenon. It also reveals interesting historical changes in the way individuality, sociability, and friendship have been constructed.

That said, change over time alone might not bear out the polarized models of premodern–modern so often constructed by historians and social scientists alike. Premodern man is often pictured as less individualistic, less self-reflexive, and more dependent on kin and local communities than modern man, who has developed a fuller individuality, and prefers intimate relationships and friends, whom he himself chooses, to wider kinship networks.[64] True, in this and the preceding chapter I see signs that development over time brings change to both subject-formation and notions of friendship. However, I have tried to nuance this observation, and sometimes even to challenge the entire premodern–modern dichotomy. As for the results of my interpretation of the different autobiographies, Rousseau in the eighteenth century was no doubt more willing to express his unique individuality than Augustine had been at the end of the fourth century, and mediaeval man may in general have been more comfortable reflecting on God, and the collective norms and values of his time, while framing his person.[65] Yet both Rousseau and Augustine emphasized the emotional element of the process of self-reflection, and both eagerly tackled the dialectic of the *ipse* and *idem* of individuality. Montaigne, although belonging to a premodern age, expressed ideas about the human character that seem almost postmodern. And none of the authors neglected the crucial part played by friends in the life and development of the individual.

All five autobiographers agree on the importance of self-reflection, of the critical examination of their own actions and motives. Albeit in different ways, they all clearly possess a capacity for self-reflexivity. Obviously, this is a talent we should not ascribe to modern man alone.

Notes

[1] See Anthony Giddens, *The Consequences of Modernity*, Cambridge, 1990; also Anthony Giddens, *Modernity and Self-Identity*, Cambridge, 1991, pp. 72 ff. See also Barbara Misztal, *Trust in Modern Societies: The Search for the Bases of Social Order*, Cambridge, 1996; Niklas Luhman, *Trust and Power*, New York, 1979.

[2] Jean-Claude Schmitt, "La decouverte de l'índividu: une fiction historiographique" in P. Mengal & F. Parot, eds., *La fabrique, la figure et la feinte: Fictions et statut des fictions en psychologie*, Paris, 1989, pp. 213–36; Aron Gurevich, *The Origins of European Individualism*, Oxford, 1995, pp. 2 ff.

[3] Georg Misch, *Geschichte der Autobiographie*, Frankfurt, 1949–62.

[4] Aron Gurevich, *The Origins of European Individualism*, Oxford, 1995, pp. 2 ff.

[5] Paul Ricoeur, *Oneself as Another*, Chicago, 1992, pp. 16 ff, 72 ff, 113–18, 140 ff.

[6] Adriana Cavarero, *Relating narratives. Storytelling and Selfhood*, London, 2000.

[7] Aristotle, *The Nicomachean Ethics*, trans. J. E. C. Welldon. New York, 1987 p. 11.

[8] Ibid., pp. 194–211, quotation p. 196.

[9] Ibid., pp. 253–254.

[10] Ibid., pp. 298–299.

[11] Michel Foucault, *The Hermeneutics of the Subject: Lectures at the Collège de France*, New York, 2004, p. 12 ff.

[12] Paul Ricoeur, *Time and narrative*, Chicago, 1984. See also Bengt Ankarloo, "Om historiens nytta," in Lars Edgren & Eva Österberg, eds., *Ut med historien!* Lund, 1992.

[13] Augustine of Hippo, *Confessions*, XI xx (26), trans. Henry Chadwick. Oxford, 1991, p. 235.

[14] Ibid., XI xxviii (37), p. 243.

[15] One can compare Augustine's thoughts here not only with Paul Ricoeur but also Reinhart Koselleck, *Vergangene Zukunft: zur Semantik geschichtliche Zeiten*, Suhrkamp, Frankfurt am Main, 1979. For an interesting discussion of time in history, see Lynn Hunt, *Measuring Time, Making History*, The Natalie Zemon Davis Annual Lectures, Central European University Press, Budapest, 2008.

[16] Augustine of Hippo, *Confessions*, VII: xii (28), trans. Henry Chadwick. Oxford, 1991, p. 244.

[17] Ibid., VII xii (28), p. 152.

[18] Peter Brown, *Augustine of Hippo: a biography*, Los Angeles, 1967, pp. 165, 169.

[19] See, for example, Claude Lorin, *Pour Saint Augustin*, Paris 1988; see also Helge Haystrup, *Augustinstudier 12: Naestekaerlighedens problematic*, Copenhagen, 2000, pp. 56 ff.

[20] Augustine of Hippo, *Confessions*, I ix (15), trans. Henry Chadwick. Oxford, 1991, p. 12.

[21] Ibid., I xx (31), p. 22.

143

[22] Ibid., II ii (7), p. 27.

[23] Ibid., II ix (17), p. 34.

[24] Ibid., II ix (17), p. 34.

[25] Ibid., III i (1), p. 35.

[26] Ibid., IV iv (7), p. 56.

[27] Ibid., IV viii (13), pp. 60–61.

[28] Ibid., VI x (17), pp. 104 ff.

[29] Ibid., VIII vii (19), p. 146.

[30] Peter Brown, *Augustine of Hippo*. London, 1967 pp. 61 ff, 158 ff, 180.

[31] Augustine of Hippo, *De civitate Dei*, XIX (3), trans. Henry Bettenson. Harmondsworth, 1984, p. 851.

[32] Ibid., XIX (5), p. 858.

[33] Ibid., XIX (8), pp. 862–3.

[34] Marie Aquinas McNamara, *Friendship in Saint Augustine*, Fribourg, 1958, pp. VII, 196 ff.

[35] Petrarch, *My secret book*, trans. John Gordon Nichols. Hesperus, 2002, p. 33.

[36] Brian McGuire, *Friendship and Community, The Monastic Experience 350–1250*, Kalamazoo, 1988, p. 424 ff; Arne Melberg, *Försök att läsa Montaigne*, Stehag, 2000, p. 55 ff.

[37] Brian McGuire, *Friendship and Community*, p. 424 ff.

[38] Michel de Montaigne, *Essays*, trans. John Florio & Charles Cotton. London, 1800, p. 229. (In Swedish, *Essayer Bok 1*, trans. Jan Stolpe. Stockholm, 1986, pp. 231–247, 311.)

[39] Arne Melberg, *Försök att läsa Montaigne*, p. 55 ff.

[40] Michel de Montaigne, *Essays*, pp. 215–216. (In Swedish, *Essayer Bok 1*, p. 238.)

[41] Michel de Montaigne, *Essayer Bok 1*, pp. 231–247, 311.

[42] Arne Melberg, *Försök att läsa Montaigne*, p. 73.

[43] Michel de Montaigne, *Essays*, pp. 201–202. (In Swedish, *Essayer Bok 1*, pp. 295–297.)

[44] Arne Melberg, *Försök att läsa Montaigne*, p. 9.

[45] Montaigne, *Essayer Bok 1*, p. 232.

[46] Michel de Montaigne, *Essays*, pp. xxi–xxii. (In Swedish, Montaigne, *Essayer Bok 1*, p. 232.)

[47] Michel de Montaigne, *Essays*, pp. 250–251. (In Swedish Montaigne, *Essayer Bok 2*, trans. Jan Stolpe. Stockholm, 1990, p. 17 ff.) For further analysis of Montaigne's views on this point see Eva Österberg, "Vännerna och jaget. Att bli individ tillsammans med andra" in Marie Lindstedt Cronberg & Catharina Stenqvist, eds., *Förmoderna livshållningar. Dygder, värden och kunskapsvägar från antiken till upplysningen*, Lund, 2008, pp. 61–62.

[48] See Paul Enoksson's preface to the Swedish translation of Giambattista Vico, *Självbiografi*, Stockholm, 1999.

[49] Natalie Zemon Davis, *The gift in sixteenth-century France*, Oxford, 2000.

[50] For thought collective see Ludwik Fleck, *Uppkomsten och utvecklingen av ett vetenskapligt faktum*, Eslöv, 1997; see also Sif Bokholm, *En kvinnoröst i manssamhället. Agda Montelius 1850–1920*, Stockholm, 2001.

[51] See Ludwik Fleck, *Uppkomsten och utvecklingen av ett vetenskapligt faktum*, Eslöv, 1997.

[52] Reinhart Koselleck, 'Einleitung', in Otto Brunner, Werner Conze & Reinhart Koselleck, eds., *Geschichtliche Grundbegriffe: historisches Lexikon zur politisch-sozialen Sprache in Deutschland*, Vol. 1. Stuttgart, 1972; Jon Helgason, *Hjärtats skrifter: En brevkulturs uttryck i korrespondensen mellan Anna Louisa Karsch och Johann Wilhelm Ludwig Gleim*, Lund, 2007, p. 35 ff.

[53] Jean-Jacques Rousseau, *Confessions*, trans. Angela Scholar. Oxford, 2000, p. 5.

[54] Ibid., p. 8.

[55] Ibid., p. 13.

[56] Ibid., pp. 96–100.

[57] Ibid., pp. 121–3.

[58] Ibid., p. 207.

[59] Ibid., p. 207.

[60] Ibid., p. 208.

[61] For example, Robert Darnton, *The Literary Underground of the Old Regime*, Cambridge, Mass., 1982.

[62] An interesting exception from most autobiographers' self-absorption is Stefan Zweig's *Die Welt von Gestern*. In what amounts to an implicit attack on Rousseau, Zweig declares at the outset that he does not see himself as being sufficiently import to be the focal point of his own account. Instead he sets out to write the history of an entire generation, a generation that like himself—Austrian, Jew, author, humanist, and pacifist—lived in a Europe rocked by the eruptions of World War II (see Eva Österberg, *Vänskap—en lång historia*, pp. 133–146).

[63] Adriana Cavarero, *Relating Narratives. Storytelling and selfhood*, London, 2000, pp. 86, 89, 92.

[64] Anthony Giddens, *The Consequences of Modernity*; Idem, *Modernity and Self-Identity. Self and Society in the Late Modern Age*.

[65] For an interesting discussion of individuality in the Middle Ages see Aron Gurevich, *The Origins of European Individualism*.

Chapter 4

Sexuality, Love, and Gender

The politics of heteronormativity in Reformation Sweden

The great narrative

As in the rest of Scandinavia, the great narrative of sixteenth- and seventeenth-century Sweden tells us about religious reformation and state-formation, defined as a process in which the State took a firm grip on fiscal and military resources, the administration of justice, and the production of ideology. After a period of Scandinavian union in the late Middle Ages, two nation states emerged to increase their grip on the population: Sweden–Finland, and Denmark–Norway.

During the latter part of the sixteenth century, Lutheran Protestantism was established as the official religion in all the Scandinavian countries; in the process, Sweden acquired a uniform national Church that has only recently been disestablished. An extremely close connection between the State and the Church grew up in which the clergy acted as state of-

147

ficials and were involved in fiscal administration, and the State looked to the Church for ideological support in policing and disciplining the people. The State operated in symbiosis with the Church; indeed, the entire culture of the period was religious–magical. The seventeenth century saw Sweden–Finland established for a time as a great power on the international scene. With King Gustavus Adolphus and his right-hand man, Axel Oxenstierna, leading the country in the first decades of the seventeenth century, Sweden–Finland became embroiled in the Thirty Years War, and engaged in vigorous empire building around the Baltic rim.

At the same time, compared with European countries such as the Dutch Republic or Britain, the striking feature of the kingdom of Sweden–Finland in this period was that it was still an overwhelmingly rural society. The nobility and the bourgeoisie constituted a tiny elite, neither amounting to more than a few per cent of the total population. Instead, over 90 per cent of the population lived in the countryside, and settlement was mostly dispersed across small villages and isolated farms. Moreover, most farms were cultivated by freeholders who, providing they paid their taxes and sent men to serve in the army when the monarch required, could tend their land and raise their families without any interference from the nobility or public officials. At the local level, they met the clergy in church, at home, at christenings, funerals, and weddings. It was a peasant culture—and a religious culture that incorporated elements from official religion and popular magical beliefs.[1]

So far so good. But what did these structures and processes actually mean for the populace? What did they imply in terms of cultural experience? What were their gendered consequences? Did they in fact have any influence on the lives of ordinary peasant households and how their close relationships functioned? To what extent and by what means did the Lutheran Church increase its control of love and sexuality in this period, which to borrow Michel Foucault's words entailed finding a new way of talking about sexuality, or rather of forbidding some types of sexuality? Which kinds of sexuality were prohibited, and with what consequences for men and women? And did the State and the Church expressly state what characterized true, legitimate love?

Foucault, for all his innovation, is rather vague when it comes to chronology, sometimes regarding the seventeenth century as the closing phase of the Middle Ages, but on other occasions as the start of a new era. However, most often it is the end of the eighteenth century that he sees as the tipping point between the older period and the modern. In the latter part of the eighteenth century, he claims, governments in Europe discovered the "population" as a resource in a whole new way: with the advent of more precise methods of data collection, and the strict registration of births and marriages, population statistics arrived to stay. In their wake, population politics threw out a great many observations concerning sex, and different discourses on sexuality materialized. In the modern period, medical science would increasingly dictate the discourse on sexuality and love, framing it in terms of what was normal or abnormal, healthy or unhealthy. Conversely, during the older period it was the law that played a similarly important role. But Foucault tries to avoid the law, for he wants to define the focus of his study in special terms: he wants to think "about sex without the law and about power without the monarch." He is intent on examining the general way of talking and thinking about sex—its discourses. In doing so, he is true to his aim of being anything but a traditional historian. However, in my view his approach is apt to underestimate the variety of discourses that can be identified in the material from early modern court proceedings. The legal material in a broad sense includes more than just the paragraphs of the law. Be it interpretations of the law, court deliberations, or legal practices, traces of different discourses—political, religious, ethical, medical, popular—are there to be unearthed.[2]

Of course, Foucault is rightly a rich source of inspiration for scholars of love and sexuality. Yet the polemic nature of his work, taken with his neglect of legal material in a broader sense and his primary focus on Catholic culture, means that the important questions about sexuality and love that he poses are well worth repeating in other contexts. The Scandinavian case presents an interesting test of his thesis in several ways: as already mentioned, the Scandinavian countries underwent a particularly effective brand of state-formation in the sixteenth and seventeenth centuries, mirrored by an extremely successful Lutheran Reformation. The Scandinavian countries, and not least Sweden–Finland, were sparsely populated, and as early as the sixteenth century the Swedish government showed great interest in controlling the population by taking measures to increase it. Thus long before the eighteenth century, many forces were at work to control people and sexual behavior to both political and moral ends.[3]

Given these facts, we would do well to reflect on why the main instruments of state-formation in post-

Reformation Sweden (the central government and the established Church) were prepared to define some forms of sexuality as a mortal sin, while others were accepted or even encouraged. It behoves us to consider whether a stricter control of human life was intended in this area, much as I have shown how early modern state-formation resulted in legislation against cronyism when it came to the administration of justice. And if so, were the restrictions effective? An interesting question is what happened to the interpretation of the law in the local and higher criminal courts when popular ideas and the defendants' beliefs encountered the arguments of the learned gentlemen of the court.

Scandinavian research has demonstrated that there was indeed such an encounter in the course of court proceedings, a kind of exchange between representatives of the people (the jury, witnesses, and so on) and the officers of the law. People met the law; they were not only victims of the workings of the law. Just as in Britain, Sweden in the seventeenth century saw a shift towards "punitive justice" and "state law" that brought with it greater control on the part of the State and better educated, more professional judges. Yet this was a gradual shift. During the whole sixteenth century and much of the seventeenth, justice in the Scandinavian countries remained a matter of negotiation, aimed at the reintegration of the delinquent into the community and compensation for the injured party, and firmly located in a local context. The goal of the legislative process was not least to achieve reconciliation and restore harmony to the community. To put it broadly, in the seventeenth century the Scandinavian countries experienced a tension between what has been called "the state-controlled expert justice" that would later come to dominate, and "the communalistic justice by negotiation" that was the traditional form of jurisprudence in the relatively homogenous Scandinavian countries.[4]

In short, when discussing sexuality, love, and control in early modern Scandinavia, I believe it is virtually impossible to "think about sex without the law and about power without the state." However, the law is far greater than the sum of its paragraphs; it embraces all the calculations in the individual cases, all the exchanges in court, and all the religious and popular ideas that influenced the law and the legal process. Similarly, no Scandinavian state can be defined as the monarch and state bureaucracy alone, but always includes the established Church, which although in some measure a separate power, was in questions of morality and close relationships a close collaborator with the State.

153

Small stories

To start complicating the issues raised by the grand narrative of early modern Scandinavia, I will match them with some small stories from Sweden that are open to interesting cultural interpretations.

The first is about Annicka Räbecka Nilsdotter, who lived in a small Swedish town in the middle of the seventeenth century. She loved a goldsmith called Anders, and they began to exchange love letters. Finally, she slept with him before they were married or even betrothed. She became pregnant and gave birth to a stillborn child. Her father was a clergyman who strongly disliked Anders. Seizing his opportunity when Annicka was devastated by the pain and grief of the birth, he forced her to promise to marry another of his own choosing: a man called Petrus who was set to become a clergyman. When Annicka recovered, she changed her mind, and remained steadfast in her love for Anders. In a letter, she wrote to Anders:

> My dearest of my heart, be assured that I will turn everything to the best; even if they should rend me asunder I will never speak anything that would deal you ill, and should I have to suffer for your

sake, yet I will wish you well, and speak well of you, my dearest, my heart.

In the end the whole sad business came to court, complete with illicit sex, broken promises, patriarchal authority, desire, and love. The remarkable outcome of this complicated lawsuit was that the lords of the court concluded that "those that loved each other should be together." They supported the girl in her love of Anders, the choice of her heart. Astonishingly, they passed a sentence that posed a direct challenge to the patriarchal authority of her father. They listened to the wishes of the woman, and upheld love and desire as valid reasons for marriage. The cathedral chapter—the relevant ecclesiastical court—agreed with the secular court: it was obvious to them that Annicka and Anders truly loved each other and wanted to live in holy matrimony, while the promises exchanged by Petrus and Annicka were made under duress from Annicka's father.[5]

In the court records we also find Sissa Jönsdotter, who in 1702 was accused of "simple fornication" with a married man. She confessed "her folly with flowing tears," as the court record puts it, and she had good reason to cry. She risked heavy fines or severe physical punishment, in her case a flogging, or a combination of the two; under canon law, she could be shamed and then excommunicated.[6]

An even more dramatic destiny awaited Ulrika Eleonora Stålhammar. She was a young woman from the lower nobility in the county of Småland. However, her family had ended up in financial difficulties. In 1713, Ulrika Eleonora left home. Once she had travelled some distance, she changed into men's clothing and severed all connections with her family. At first she went to Stockholm, the capital, hoping to become a soldier. Her situation was precarious for some time until—still as a man—she got a job as a servant in a series of fine households, under the name of Wilhelm Edstedt. In 1715, however, we find her in the small town of Kalmar, where she became a soldier at last. Pretending to be a man, she even married a woman, Maria Lönman. In 1729, however, she revealed her true identity, and was put on trial in the district court in Kalmar, along with her wife. Both were accused of having deceived the Church into sanctioning their marriage, and Ulrika Eleonora was also accused of having deceived the army.

During the trial it was revealed that after a while Ulrika Eleonora had told Maria that she was not "a true man," yet they had continued to live together. Several witnesses attested to the couple's godly, sober and loving life. In fact, several testified that Ulrika Eleonora on the face of it performed her duties as a soldier well, and led an exemplary private life. There was not a bad word to be said about either her or Maria.

The case was referred to the appellate court, where the judges were not slow to identify the laws under which Ulrika Eleonora could be condemned to death. She had "changed her sex," and that alone was "an abomination in the eyes of God." Moreover, she and Maria had married, and thus defiled a sacrament of the Church. Yet astonishingly, the sentences the court handed down on both charges were mild. Ulrika Eleonora was sentenced to one month's imprisonment on bread and water, public penance, and expulsion from the town of Kalmar; Maria to fourteen days' imprisonment.[7]

How to interpret the fates of these different women? We are confronted with two extremely independent women, who broke with the prevailing norms but nevertheless managed to escape the worst punishment: Annicka, mother of an illegitimate, stillborn child, who persuaded the gentlemen of the court and the Church that her love for Anders was true; and Ulrika Eleonora, self-appointed soldier and loving husband. Yet we are also confronted with the likes of Sissa, who was punished without mercy for having had sex with a married man.

What connections are there between the single grand narrative and the innumerable small stories, between power, politics, and religious transformation on the one hand and the fates of women and men from all walks of life on the other? Was it the case that this period of indoctrination, state-formation, and war saw the definitions of love and sexuality renegotiated, or perhaps even explicitly reformulated, and a whole series of ethical practices reinvented? The equally pressing corollary is whether, in relation to men, the situation of women deteriorated as a result.

The international debate

Many well-known scholars, such as Lyndal Roper, have argued that the Reformation itself was gendered, as was the whole of society after the Reformation generally speaking. According to most European and American scholars—Lawrence Stone, Renate Bridenthal, Merry Wiesner, Gerda Lerner and others—state-formation, the Reformation, and early modern capitalism mostly had a negative impact on women. As Merry E. Wiesner has put it, it was unfortunate that it was to be occupations with formal education, political functions, capital, and international contacts—that is, merchants, bankers, doctors, senior civil servants, and officers—that achieved wealth, power, and prestige at this time. Women were excluded. Forging a world economy, fighting wars; these were male affairs.[8] Women were handicapped by their lack of education and mobility.

The general picture was the same in the seventeenth century. The Reformation, both as a credo and as a social movement, in Lyndal Roper's view should be understood as a "gender theory." For women, the legacy of Protestantism was profoundly ambivalent. In its institutionalized form, the Lutheran Reformation meant that little encouragement was given to women's independent spirituality; far less than in the Catholic Middle Ages. Instead, the Lutheran Reformation ushered in a notion that women should be firmly confined to the household, subordinate to men. The Reformation staked out its own particular view of marriage, sexuality, and prostitution, and it was in this process that gender became decisive, in both ideological and real terms.[9]

It has been argued that neither the Protestant Reformation nor the Catholic Counter-Reformation brought any improvement to the position of women. Only some utopian groups such as the Baptists or the

Quakers pleaded for the equality of the sexes. Otherwise, patriarchy was only strengthened in the seventeenth century. The witch trials of the period 1500–1750 saw as many as 100,000 Europeans brought before the courts, and perhaps a third of the accused executed. The vast majority of the victims were women, often elderly women.[10]

Other historians, it is true, have been sceptical of the significance of religious ideas in determining real relationships between men and women. The realities of life in small households compelled the formation of more equal relationships, with a shared responsibility for both family and work, it has been suggested. Cultural historians such as Natalie Zemon Davis make a point of the variety and ambivalence of women's situations in these centuries, without laying claim to an all-purpose explanation in terms of religion or iniquitous gender contracts.[11]

Nevertheless, the prevailing view is that the Reformation brought fresh disadvantages for women. The picture painted by international research is generally bleak. The key social processes in the sixteenth and seventeenth centuries—the emergence of the military state, bureaucratization, early capitalism, the increased demand for formal education, the Protestant Reformation, and rationalistic philosophy—are

160

supposed to have meant a general worsening in their situation. State, Church, and science alike supported the patriarchal ideology. This forced women to retreat further into the home and the private sphere. At the same time, the authorities tightened their control of sexuality; it was only to be practiced within marriage.

The question is the extent to which this general thesis is valid for Scandinavian conditions. The international picture has sometimes been painted in very broad strokes, with generalizations applied to large parts of Europe over periods of a century or more. Where it is supported by empirical data, the sources tend to be taken mostly from France, Germany, or Britain. There is in my view reason to reserve judgement on whether it is applicable to an agrarian society such as Sweden. Therefore, let us look more closely into the Swedish case, maintaining our particular focus on sexuality and love. In doing so, I hope to muddy the general picture somewhat, while making sense of those small stories in a way that remains true to their full complexity.

Church, State, and sexuality in post-Reformation Sweden

As we have seen, the State and the established Church were the major forces behind the discourses of love and sexuality in Sweden, just as in the rest of Scandinavia in the early modern period. But there are two aspects to observe: the influence of the State was not solely restricted to exercise of the law; neither was Church control only visible in its penalties. Both State and Church had other channels of communication, and both met the people in a variety of contexts.

For the representatives of the Church, the main opportunities were sermons and homilies at baptisms, weddings, and funeral, all occasions when the Church implicitly or explicitly could present its ideas about how women and men should behave within matrimony, or how the ideal version of a happy, loving marriage was constructed. Let us look more closely at the official religious discourse as it is represented in the homilies given by Swedish bishops and clergy. In 1682 a clergyman's wife was buried. She was 47 years old at her death, with twenty-four years of marriage and sixteen children behind her. The clergyman who presided at her burial spoke of her in the following terms:

Her beloved husband she waited on as any wife in the world would have done. Loved and honored him from her heart, and never tired of serving him, both in good times and in bad. She strove to make all his days pleasant, never disagreeable. She followed his counsel—what pleased him, pleased her. … She kept the household as an honest wife, nor let pass a moment when she could keep it in order. Of the household she was always the first up and last to bed, tending to her domestic duties, putting the servants to work, and seeing that they had their food and wages in good time. … She has been the faithful support of her household in her housekeeping, dealings, and conduct.[12]

This is typical of how the ideal woman's role was set out in seventeenth-century funeral sermons and eulogies. They are, of course, stereotyped, and insufficient as evidence of the way people really behaved. But the very fact of their repetitions and recurrent phrases shows how the Church *wanted* people to live their lives. They were intended to teach people the art of living a good life, and likewise the art of making a good death. In truth, they add up to a fascinating material, only now being fully used in modern research; an unexpectedly rich source of ideas of masculinity and femininity, of virtue and sin, of suffering and subordination.

To summarize the general message conveyed in these funeral sermons and eulogies, it is obvious that the Church's ideal was that a woman should be married, and that as a wife she should be a "pillar of the household." She ought to be humble towards practically everyone; honest, loyal and loving towards her husband; and orderly and responsible in her everyday tasks: the same themes appear again and again. And yet it should be noted that the ideal of womanly virtue so expressed was largely identical to the ideal of male virtue. Fear of God was a common strand, as were caring for the home and loving each other. The notion of the social roles of the sexes was embedded in a mode of discourse that above all spoke of God, honor, virtue, and the well-being of the whole household. Spouses were supposed to love each other, trust and care for each other, take care of the children, look to the poor, and so on. But while the female virtues stopped dead at the front door, the male sphere stretched out to include public business and the wider world.[13]

The reverse of the Church's ideal woman was the witch. In the big witch trials in the Swedish regions of Dalarna, Hälsingland, Ångermanland, and Gästrikland in the years 1668–1675, a total of 856 people were accused of joining in witches' rides to celebrate the witches' Sabbath on the island of Blåkulla, abducting children for the Devil, or working black magic on people or livestock. Only 116, or 14 per cent, of the accused were men. The rest were women, often elderly, often—but not always—poor. The courts only reinforced this hostility to women; proportionately there were more women than men amongst those sentenced to death, and amongst the 240 or so people who were actually executed.[14]

Life on Blåkulla as described in the court record was rather merry at times. People dance, eat, drink, and have sex just as they do at home in the village, with the difference that here things are topsy-turvy. They have sex, for example, back to back. Old women, however, are sometimes treated in a humiliating way in these tales: they were turned upside down to serve as candelabra, with candles stuck in their bottoms and genitals, to illuminate the wild parties.[15]

However, it should be born in mind that the witch trials were unparalleled in the history of Swedish justice. In their most bloody and absurd form, witch trials were a phenomenon that was largely confined to a few decades; outside that period, while there were certainly other examples of the prosecution of folk beliefs and superstitions, they did not have the lethal consequences of the great witch trials. More often people were brought to court on less sensational charges. In the sixteenth century, different kinds of violence, normally between men, dominated. But in the seventeenth century a different class of crime became increasingly common, one that reveals the State and Church's ambitions to control sexuality.[16]

From the start, the Lutheran Reformation had tended to venerate marriage, and gradually the boundaries of sexuality sanctioned by Church and State were drawn in ever tighter. In 1608 the National Law was changed to include sections from the Ten Commandments, increasing the punishments for several kinds of prohibited sexuality, indeed for almost any conceivable kind of sexuality outside marriage.

It should be underlined that the sexual deviance cases that came to court only rarely included rape. Most often the cases concerned sex outside marriage. What we glimpse in the court records—the great witchcraft cases excepted—is hardly a period of violent sexual expression or brutal violence against women. Rather we must interpret the sources as showing that there were powers at work that tried to maintain the sanctity of marriage and teach people sexual fidelity, determined to prevent the illegitimate children who would become a burden on the parish. The law, the Church, and state officials, with the backing of at least the leading representatives of the peasantry, collaborated to support this norm—a norm that was shared by many people in traditional peasant communities.[17]

As a result of this legislation, which had its parallels in all the other Scandinavian countries, thousands upon thousands of women and men were dragged before the courts and endured severe punishments for one thing, and one thing only. They were condemned for what we today consider to be our own private business: they had slept together without being married or betrothed. They could be flogged, pay heavy fines, or be shamed in church. Some men and women were even condemned to death for what was called "double fornication," or adultery when both parties were married. In most cases, however, the death penalty was not actually carried out. It has been shown that in the middle of the seventeenth century, the death sentence was commuted to a fine, banishment, or corporal punishment in more than 70 per cent of the cases heard in one of the Swedish high courts.[18]

The courts viewed cases of "single fornication," when only one party was married, somewhat more leniently, but it was still embarrassing, wrong, and a threat to society. The girl Sissa, whom I mentioned above, had slept with a married man. She had every reason to stand before the court with "flowing tears." She had disgraced herself and lost her honor as a woman because she had committed the great sin of the age: she had enjoyed physical love outside marriage.

Within marriage, on the other hand, sexuality was welcome. That was considered healthy sexuality, encouraged by Luther himself. Both men and women had the right to enjoy each other's bodies. In this respect there was no prudery in post-Reformation Scandinavia. By these lights it was merely prudent for the judge and cathedral chapter to be influenced by Annicka Räbecka's love letters to her beloved Anders, and by her outspoken longing for him. It is obvious that a discourse of love already existed—long before the nineteenth-century, middle-class family ideal with its reverence for romantic love. Annicka and Anders' letters reveal that much. And the authorities realized this. If people who loved and desired each other could also be together, there was a good chance that the marriage would survive, and both parties would be happy and loyal. The upshot of the court's reasoning was that they would choose to support the young lovers and respect the girl's wishes, even if it meant opposing her father.

But what of Ulrika Eleonora, with her men's clothing and her Maria, her wife? Why was she let off a flogging and a long prison sentence, although the marriage between two women was an outrage in the eyes of the Church? In fact, the 1608 Supplementary Law had for the first time introduced in a secular Swedish law a clear proscription against homosexuality. But the paragraph was directed against men: "you shall not lie close to a man in the same manner as you lie close to a women; if you do, you are both condemned to death and your blood shall be shed." To the mystification of later historians, this paragraph was removed from the National Law the next time it was revised, in the 1730s. Reading the parliamentary records of the time, we can see that the legal experts took a novel line: let us not have this paragraph any more, in which we make this horrible crime explicit. Rather, let us speak as little as possible about homosexuality; perhaps it might even disappear if no one talks about it. On the other hand, if we make it a visible problem and talk about it, this abomination might spread. This seems to have been their argument, according to an analysis of the legal discourses.[19]

So, in 1608 a paragraph was inserted in the Secular Law directed against male homosexuality, while legal experts hundred years later chose a strategy of silence. Later, in 1864, the paragraph was reintroduced at the same time as lesbian love was explicitly forbidden. It took almost another hundred years until same-sex love between adults was permitted under Swedish law in the 1940s, for men as well as women.

How then was this paragraph applied between 1608 and 1734? The answer is, very rarely. There were very few trials for homosexuality in the Nordic countries in the early modern period. In Sweden it has been calculated that no more than some twenty such cases were heard in the courts between c.1600 and 1750. Only very exceptionally did courts hear cases concerning women wearing men's clothing, potential cases of lesbian relationships. On the other hand, in the seventeenth and eighteenth centuries close to 1,000 Swedish men were executed for bestiality. And it can be estimated that at least 10,000–20,000 men and women were put on trial for fornication or adultery in the same period. These rough numbers clearly show that it was illicit sexuality between adult men and women that was the focus of the prescriptive discourse of the time.[20]

The main impression, then, is that homosexuality was rarely prosecuted in the Nordic countries at this point. There may be a number of reasons for this. Evidence was always a difficult matter, and according to the procedural rules, accusations that could not be verified were turned against the accuser. Thus it was risky to accuse someone of such a serious offence. Moreover, and in my view more importantly, State and Church surveillance was far more concerned with ensuring that only legitimate children conceived in wedlock were born. Post-Reformation trials generally concentrated on the threats to public decency rather than on clandestine sexual practices that did not result in pregnancy. This preoccupation with sanctioned reproduction was also the reason why more men were put on trial for bestiality than for sexual relations with other men: homosexuality did not produce children and therefore was not considered so very dangerous after all; while the popular mentality of the period admitted of the notion that intercourse between man and animal might result in the birth of something half-human. A calf with a human face was a frightening thought in the popular mind.[21]

When it came to lesbian relationships the law was less explicit, as I have mentioned. It was for this reason that Ulrika Eleonora could be treated leniently, especially as she was careful to appear respectful and submissive in court, and she mobilized her influential family to come to her assistance. In this period, society's dread of immorality and sin, it seems, was not primarily constructed around homosexuality. What was feared most were extramarital sexuality and illegitimate children, who could only complicate the patterns of inheritance and landownership.

For State and Church alike, good order meant heterosexuality, harmonious marriages based on true love, legitimate children brought up in respectable agrarian households, farmers paying their taxes, and everyone going to church. Obviously, what law and religion agreed to construct was holy matrimony. In Scandinavia, it seems that this was done more effectively than in any other region in Europe at the time, apart perhaps from Scotland—even if the same tendencies can be seen across northern Europe and in the Puritan colonies in America. But in the Scandinavian case, the Lutheran Reformation had seen the king become head of the Church. As a result, the Church lost most of its legal powers to the secular courts, and the laws on sexual morality seem to have become particularly rigorous in the Nordic countries; this much is evident from the crime statistics. In the middle of the seventeenth century in much of southern Sweden, for example, sexual crimes accounted for some 40 per cent of the total.[22] Most of the cases concerned sex outside marriage: "double adultery," "single adultery," or simply fornication between the unmarried.

Thus, as a part of state-formation, fundamentalist Lutheranism in early modern Sweden had a control on sexuality that was remarkable for the period, with much the same penalties, including flogging and death sentences, as we can find in other fundamentalist countries much later in history. However, the prohibitions were combined with a more positive message: the message that the authorities respected what they saw as true love, and supported the idea of matrimony as a mutual, life-long, loving responsibility. In my view, the consequences for women of this combined discourse of prohibition on extramarital sexuality and support of honest love were somewhat ambivalent. In fact, the same goes for the general ideological and educational effects of the Reformation. It is in this context that I wish to turn to some of the other issues involved.

Firstly, it is important that both sexes were equally

subject to the same, strict control of their sexuality, even if the penalties meted out were not always similar. The main point is that the control of illicit sexuality was indeed strict, regardless of gender. Was this negative or positive for women? Today we may well be outraged to read how poor, unmarried young men and women had to face humiliation in court and heavy fines for extramarital sex. Yet for some women it must have been a distinct advantage that society's norms helped them compel the men who had made them pregnant to marry them. This was in fact what often happened in court. And popular norms and the judicial process could at least force the man to admit paternity, even if it did not result in marriage. For example, it has been shown that it was unusual in rural southern Sweden for a child to be born without an acknowledged father in the period up to the end of the eighteenth century. Certainly, illegitimate children were born, but their fathers at least acknowledged their paternity.[23] In contrast, when extramarital sexuality was later decriminalized in the nineteenth century, a great many children were born without their fathers taking any responsibility at all. It is thus my belief that the strict sexual norms of the post-Reformation period were more general than gendered. Their object was sanctioned reproduction, a fruitful household; their means the control of both men and women.

In terms of gender patterns, it should also be remembered that women appeared in court quite often, and not only in cases of sexual offences. They frequently turn up as witnesses, and even as party to financial cases. It is obvious that women in Scandinavia in this period had a much greater legal standing than previous research supposed. They stood before the court as independent individuals, far more so than you might expect given the prevailing patriarchal ideology.[24]

We should also consider the extent of popular participation in those social and ritual occasions when the Church appeared in another light than when lending its support to the State in controlling morality. Using ritual bonds such as godparenting to reveal social relationships, Julie Hardwick has demonstrated, that between 1560 and 1660 only 10 per cent of godparents among civil servants in Nantes in France were women. Hardwick makes quite a point of this. She argues that "men's claiming of the public celebration of a child's birth reflected and reinforced the associations between gender and authority that pervaded early modern society."[25] Interestingly, however, findings in Sweden show quite another pattern;

here women were much more likely to stand godparent. For example, in the city of Gothenburg between 1655 and 1673, the godparents were 47 per cent women and 53 per cent men. In the city of Helsingborg between 1680 and 1709, women were in the majority, at 55 per cent.[26] Thus, whatever the reason, there is no parallel to Hardwick's result here. The Swedish findings instead imply that women were active participants in social networks—not least in forming religious ties, and in church rituals. Thus not only did women participate actively in the courts, they also operated in religious arenas as independent actors.

The education of women is also revealing. The sermons and eulogies read at women's funerals did not limit their praise to the women's obedience, piety, and loving care. The bishop of Linköping, for example, also stressed how praiseworthy it was that women had learned to read and write, and even in some cases to count.[27] The Church Law of 1686 had assigned the clergy the task of carefully assessing people's knowledge of religion all over Sweden, every year, and of registering all the members of the households. Many people learned to read as a result of the clergy visiting their houses. For example, it has been calculated that 74 per cent of the population in a parish in the north of Sweden in 1691 had elementary reading skills, a figure that a few decades later rose to over 80 per cent. On the other hand, people did not learn to write to the same extent.

As several historians have pointed out, we should not have any illusions about what this literacy meant—it certainly did not mean the same kind of quick reading capacity usual today, when many race through novels and detective stories for relaxation. What the average Swede attained in the latter part of the seventeenth century was, as it has been put, "literacy for domestic religious needs." In virtually every household there were one or two people who could read aloud from the Bible or the catechism, and one or more others who could plod through them or who had learned them by heart. This was only the beginnings of literacy as we understand the term today, but it was significant. And, it should be noted, no gender distinctions here! The clergy examined the girls' literacy just like the boys'. Religious education and social control of the household touched women and men alike, and all of them might benefit from such indoctrination for the opportunity to acquire certain basic skills.[28]

This conclusion seems quite surprising in an international comparison. Gerda Lerner has claimed that in the early modern period in most European countries, women were less capable of reading than men: in Scotland, for example, some 70 per cent of men were literate in the period 1630–1760, as opposed to only 20 per cent of women; in England, 64 per cent of men and only 26 per cent of the women could read in the middle of the eighteenth century.[29] Sweden's high literacy figures as early as the seventeenth century are astonishing as an indication of effective Church control and the education of both men and women.

Control and ambivalence

Drawing on the different aspects of the Swedish—and to a large extent Scandinavian—experience in the post-Reformation period, I will conclude by suggesting that women generally faced an ambivalent and varied situation. It means that in the international debate, I join with scholars such as Natalie Zemon Davis and Arlette Farge in stressing cultural variety, rather than with those who single out women's generally increasing subordination in the early modern period.[30]

The Swedish case presents a striking example of the combined efforts of the State and the Protestant

Church in achieving a fundamentalist control of sexuality, permitting sex within heterosexual marriage and, sometimes mercifully, between betrothed persons intended to build a family—but then and only then. However, this central control did not only hold women within the confines of marriage and the heterosexual imperative, it also constrained men. The instrument of continuous control presented by the clergy as the state's officials also contributed to a tremendous increase in literacy, for both men and women.

It is reasonable to suggest that Sweden's relative cultural homogeneity, combined with the sparseness of its population and a social structure in which a majority of farms were small or middle-sized, were contributing factors. The realities of life in small households encouraged the formation of more equal relationships, with shared responsibility for both family and work. It is my contention that the Reformation in Sweden saw not the creation of patriarchy pure and simple, but rather a hierarchical power system that amounted to a milder form of patriarchy based on reciprocity, mutual obligations, and care. Make no mistake, the man was the head of the household and had greater liberty to act outside its confines. But gender was embedded in a discourse of

God, law, household, honor, and sanctioned sexuality, which allowed many men to consider their wives their best friends and companions, and safeguarded the well-being of the mutual household. And in most cases it seems both men and women supported the norms that let love's voice be heard when settling a marriage, or that kept young and old alike faithful to their wedding vows.

The Lutheran Reformation in Sweden, defined as a process of social control pursued by the State and the Church in combination, was thus in my view not about sexuality per se—there were many kinds of sexuality that went more or less neglected, after all. Neither was it about women's sexuality alone. Rather, it was about matrimony and sanctioned forms of reproduction. This made sense in a country with a small population, and made for good fiscal policy on the part of a government that was so heavily dependent on taxes—and drafted soldiers—from farmers' households. The God-given order was a construction that allowed for love, lust, and desire, but only within the exclusive confines of heteronormativity. The God-given order embedded a gender discourse in the general discourse of the household, possibly blurring both in the process. In Sweden's grand narrative, the household can serve as a metaphor for the central government or the royal court. In the many small stories, the household was both a fundamental reality and a symbol of happiness, decency, and honor.

Intolerant rules and cruel restrictions were also no doubt part of the discourse of sexuality and love in seventeenth-century Sweden, just as Foucault has argued for other parts of Europe. However, legislative restrictions were not the sum total of the prescriptive discourse—and neither was criminalization the only ideological instrument available to the authorities. From the pulpit and in their regular meetings with peasant households, the Protestant clergy preached the positive values of matrimony, of harmonious relations between men and women, of true love, and the right and proper sexuality within marriage. And in the courts, professional interpretations of the law interacted with popular and religious notions to fashion a discourse that not only seemed reasonable to the early modern State, but also spoke to many people in the rural communities of the day.

Notes

[1] Göran Behre, Lars-Olof Larsson & Eva Österberg, *Sveriges historia 1521–1809: Stormaktsdröm och småstatsrealitet*, Stockholm, 2001.

[2] Michel Foucault, *Historie de la sexualité I: La volonté de savoir*, Paris, 1976. For a more complex view of legal practice and the law, and the different discourses that may be traced in court records see, for example, Eva Österberg & Sölvi Bauge Sogner, *People Meet the Law: Control and Conflict-handling in the Courts*, Oslo, 2000; Eva Bergenlöv, *Skuld och oskuld. Barnamord och barnkvävning i rättslig diskurs och praxis omkring 1680–1800*, Lund, 2004; Christopher Collstedt, *Duellanten och rättvisan: Duellbrott och synen på manlighet i stormaktsväldets slutskede*, Lund, 2007.

[3] See, for example, Eva Österberg, *Kolonisation och kriser*, Lund, 1977, pp. 132–144.

[4] See Douglas Hay, "Property, Authority, and the Criminal Law" in D. Hay, P. Linebaugh & E. P. Thompson, eds., *Albion's Fatal Tree: Crime and Society in Eighteenth-Century England*, London, 1975. See also Eva Österberg & Erling Sandmo, "Introduction," in Eva Österberg & Sölvi Bauge Sogner, eds., *People Meet the Law: Control and Conflict-handling in the courts*, Oslo, 2000, pp. 9–26.

[5] My former student Malin Lennartsson found and analyzed this remarkable case in her excellent doctoral thesis (Malin Lennartsson, *I Säng och sate*, Lund, 1999, pp. 177–181).

[6] This court case is analyzed in Marie Lindstedt Cronberg, *Synd och skam: Ogifta mödrar på svensk landsbygd 1680–1880*, Lund, 1997.

[7] See Eva Österberg, "Förbjuden kärlek och förtigandets strategi. När Ulrika Eleonora gifte sig med Maria," in Eva Österberg, ed., *Jämmerdal och fröjdesal. Kvinnor i stormaktsti-*

182

dens Sverige. Stockholm, 1997, pp. 267–283. See also Lars-Olof Larsson, *På marsch mot evigheten. Svensk stormaktstid i släkten Stålhammars spegel,* Stockholm 2007, pp. 281–298. For other research on women in men's clothing in the same period, see Rudolf Dekker & Lotte van de Pol, *Vrouwen in mannenkleren,* Amsterdam, 1989.

[8] For example Merry E. Wiesner, "Spinning out capital. Women's Work in Early Modern Economy," in Renate Bridenthal, Claudia Koontz & Susan Stuard, eds., *Becoming visible. Women in European History.* Boston 1987.

[9] Lyndal Roper, *The Holy Household: Women and Morals in Reformation Augsburg,* Oxford, 1989.

[10] See, for example, Bengt Ankarloo & Gustav Henningsen, eds., *Häxornas Europa 1400–1700,* Lund, 1987; and William Monter, "Protestant Wives, Catholic Saints, and the Devil's Handmaid: Women in the Age of Renaissance" in Renate Bridenthal, Claudia Koontz & Susan Stuard, eds., *Becoming Visible: Women in European History,* Boston, 1987.

[11] See, for example, Natalie Zemon Davis & Arlette Farge, *A History of Women: Renaissance and Enlightenment Paradoxes,* Cambridge, Mass., 1993.

[12] For these and other similar examples, see Barbro Bergner, "Dygden som levnadskonst. Kvinnliga dygdeideal under stormaktstiden," in Eva Österberg, ed., *Jämmerdal och fröjdesal,* pp. 71–124.

[13] Ibid., p. 76 ff.

[14] Bengt Ankarloo, *Trolldomsprocesserna i Sverige,* Rättshistoriskt bibliotek, Lund, 1971, pp. 113–314.

[15] Ibid., pp. 217–223.

[16] For crime patterns in Sweden and other Scandinavian countries in the early modern period see, for example, Eva

Österberg & Dag Lindström, *Crime and Social Control in Medieval and Early Modern Swedish Towns*, Uppsala, 1988; Eva Österberg, "Social Arena or Theatre of Power? The Courts, Crime, and the Early Modern State in Sweden," in Heikki Pihlajamäki, ed., *Theatres of Power. Social Control and Criminality in Historical Perspective*, Jyväskylä, 1991, pp. 8–25; Eva Österberg & Sölvi Bauge Sogner, eds., *People Meet the Law. Control and Conflict-handling in the Courts*, Oslo, 2000.

[17] For crime patterns see Eva Österberg & Sölvi Bauge Sogner, eds., *People Meet the Law*.

[18] Rudolf Thunander, *Hovrätt i funktion: Göta hovrätt och brottmålen 1635–1699*, Stockholm, 1993, p. 88. See also Hans Eyvind Naess & Eva Österberg, "Sanctions, Agreements. Sufferings," in Eva Österberg & Sölvi Bauge Sogner, eds., *People Meet the Law*, pp. 140–166.

[19] See Jonas Liliequist, "Staten och sodomiten—tystnaden kring homosexuella handlingar i 1600- och 1700-talens Sverige," in *Lambda nordica*, Vol. 1, 1995, Stockholm. See also Eva Österberg, "Förbjuden kärlek och förtigandets strategi. När Ulrika Eleonora gifte sig med Maria" in Eva Österberg, ed., *Jämmerdal och fröjdesal*, pp. 267–283.

[20] The basis for estimations such as this can be found in Eva Österberg & Sölvi Bauge Sogner, eds., *People Meet the Law*.

[21] See, for example, Jonas Liliequist, *Brott, synd och straff. Tidelagsbrottet i Sverige under 1600- och 1700-talen*, Umeå, 1992; and Jonas Liliequist, "Peasants against Nature. Crossing the Boundaries between Man and Animal in Seventeenth and Eighteenth Century Sweden," in *Journal of the History of Sexuality*, Vol. 1 No.3, 1991.

[22] See Eva Österberg & Sölvi Bauge Sogner, eds., *People Meet the Law*, p. 84 ff, 181 ff.

184

[23] Marie Lindstedt Cronberg, *Synd och skam. Ogifta mödrar på svensk landsbygd 1680–1880*, Lund, 1997.

[24] See Sölvi Bauge Sogner, Marie Lindstedt Cronberg & Hilde Sandvik, "Women in Court," in Eva Österberg & Sölvi Bauge Sogner, eds., *People Meet the Law*, pp. 167–201.

[25] Julie Hardwick, *The Practice of Patriarchy. Gender and the Politics of Household in Early Modern France*. Philadelphia, 1998, p. 180.

[26] See Solveig Fagerlund, *Handel och Vandel. Vardagslivets sociala struktur ur ett kvinnoperspektiv, Helsingborg ca 1680–1709.* Lund, 2002, p. 54.

[27] See Eva Österberg, *Folk förr. Historiska essäer*, pp. 215–216; Barbro Bergner, "Dygden som levnadskonst. Kvinnliga dygdeideal under stormaktstiden," in Eva Österberg, ed., *Jämmerdal och fröjdesal*, pp. 71–124.

[28] See for a discussion of the Scandinavian findings, in English, Loftur Guttormsson, "The Development of Popular Religious Literacy in the Seventeenth and Eighteenth Century," in *Scandinavian Journal of History* 1990:1, Stockholm, 1990.

[29] Gerda Lerner, *The Creation of Feminist Consciousness from the Middle Ages to Eighteen-seventy*, Oxford, 1994, p. 10.

[30] See, for example, Natalie Zemon Davis & Arlette Farge, *A History of Women. Renaissance and Enlightenment Paradoxes*, Cambridge, Mass., 1993.

Chapter 5

Close Relationships—Then and Now

Ethics and politics

In the previous chapters I set out to show how pre-modern love and friendship, both as ideals and in the full diversity of reality, were not only important in private life, but also in public life. The focus of my analysis has been the ways that philosophers, writers, and State and Church thought and spoke about close relationships, and the great changes in these discourses over time. But I have also been able to shed light on specific variations in actual relationships by using diaries, correspondence, and autobiographical material. It goes without saying that I have only been able to touch upon a fraction of the cultural variations according to gender, class, generation, ethnicity, and so on that in all likelihood distinguished love and friendship in their authentic historical expression.

187

Both love and friendship were a part of what the classical philosophers termed *philia* (in Greek) or *amicitia* (in Latin). Friendship was defined by *reciprocity*, *trust*, *voluntariness*, and at the very least a stab at *equality*. Love comprised much the same ingredients, above all trust and reciprocity. But it was also based upon sexuality or the "natural" ties between parents and children or siblings. Close relationships such as friendship and love could at their best give comfort and joy; they were, and are, existentially indispensable. Yet for the classical authorities there was more: *philia* could also bring tangible benefits. Ultimately, the perfect friendship between two good men would lead to increased self-knowledge and a degree of virtue and integrity that could only enrich society, according to Aristotle. As later philosophers would emphasize in turn, friendship in classical philosophy was less a matter of emotion and psychology than of ethics and justice—and thus of politics.

Classical philosophies of friendship thus saw both the ideal of *philia* and actual close relationships as intruding on the spheres of public life, politics, ethics, and subject-formation. The language and narratives of friendship have consequently played an important role both in political speech and in autobiographical accounts of individual development in the older period. I have touched on this with the example of Swedish political rhetoric from the seventeenth century, and an analysis of a number of significant autobiographies from the mediaeval and early modern period (Augustine, Petrarch, Montaigne, Vico, Rousseau). The autobiographies show that friends have always played a role in individual development, but also that friendship's province and function is construed differently according to the writer's historical context and the purpose of the narrative.

Because in the older period close relationships were held to be part of a larger ethical and political sphere, friendship and love–sexuality have had a tendency to appear dangerous to the authorities in some periods, so much so that they often think them best controlled, regulated, or restricted. I have discussed this by drawing on examples of ambivalent mediaeval views on monastic friendship, of state intervention against cronyism in the early modern period, and of the Church and State's combined control of love and sexuality in seventeenth-century, post-Reformation Sweden.

* * *

What then are the general conclusions to be drawn? Even if the existential need for close relationships transcends time, the contours of friendship and sexuality in the real world, and accepted notions of their nature, are culturally determined and are thus subject to a variation. But there are some things that have changed dramatically, while others seem to remain relatively unaltered despite centuries of Western culture. Take the fact that I have yet to find an example of friendship, in thought or deed, that deviates from certain fundamental elements of the classical definition of *philia*. Be it Aristotle, Cicero, Montaigne, Queen Christina, an English priest, or an early modern merchant, they all to some degree argue that you choose your own friends, and expect loyalty, mutual kindness, and trust in return. In this respect, the ethical demands of good friendship have altered little in the periods I have considered.

Other elements have changed over time, however. In the old philosophy of friendship, there was also an idea that ideal friendship could best be realized if the parties were equal, or at any rate almost on a par with each other. On this point there has been a considerable difference of opinion ever since. In the Middle Ages and the sixteenth and seventeenth centuries, the language and gestures of friendship were also employed in unequal relationships: between old and young, regent and courtier, and so on. The dividing line with what perhaps ought to be termed patron–client relationships was often indistinct. Patron–client relationships are meant to incline towards the informal, personal, and reciprocal, but nevertheless clearly hierarchical, while friendship is meant to be informal, personal, reciprocal, and, with a bit of luck, equal besides. Yet my analyses of mediaeval Icelandic sagas and early modern correspondence and diaries have shown that what people then termed friendship networks were just as likely to consist of unequal relationships. In their day they constituted necessary social alliances, alliances that transcended the boundary between private and public.

Greek *philia* and Latin *amicitia* both encompassed what we would think of as familial love. But the relationship that most interested the classical philosophers was the "perfect friendship." It correlated with strength of character and wisdom, and good men, in attaining it, would communicate its principles into the political sphere, to the benefit of all. Classical ideas were adopted in the Middle Ages by Christian thinkers such as Augustine in the fourth century, Aelred of Rievaulx in the twelfth century, and Bernard of Clairvaux at the turn of the twelfth century, and converted—literally—into the idea of a spiritual friendship intent on union with God. The ideal friend was now a *custos animi*, a guardian of his friend's soul who safeguards his spiritual development. Here too friendship had a higher purpose than providing pleasant company.

Friendship in the older period transcended boundaries, for it belonged both in the private and the public spheres, as I have argued. Friendship demanded action—an English merchant had to take sides, an Icelandic farmer had promises to live up to—and in this it was just as much public as private. Friendship was also an important political term in the language rulers used with their subjects in the seventeenth century. It signified peace and alliances with other powers.

All that would change later. Broadly speaking, friendship, like love between adults, came increasingly to inhabit the private sphere according to the discourses of the nineteenth and twentieth centuries. What happened en route to modern society was that the ideal friendship that once aspired to greater things—the greater good, or God—tended to become an end in itself, a concern for the people directly involved, but scarcely any higher purpose. In its modern outline, as summed up in the twentieth century by the sociologist Alberoni amongst others, friendship lies to one side of politics, to one side of family life. Friendship is private, elective, reciprocal, and trustful. Both friendship and love are elements in a necessary antithesis to public life in the modern world, states Alan Silver.[1] It is true that when women were still denied political suffrage at the start of the twentieth century, for example, they turned to private relationships to mobilize their forces to political ends. Yet this rather proves the point; modern demarcation lines between private and public had been established by men in authority, and in their attempt to cross them, women were forced to exploit their personal contacts to the full.[2]

The other difference if we compare Aristotle's argument with twentieth-century definitions, is that the boundary between love and friendship had gradually become more distinct. Aristotle did not differentiate sharply between the two. He could contemplate the idea of friendship having an erotic component.[3] Even much later, romantic and sensual friendship could be articulated in literature and private correspondence without it being thought problematic.[4] Yet eventually love would increasingly be defined as a unique and strong feeling, expressed in part in sexual compatibility. Friendship, meanwhile, to borrow Al-

193

beroni's words, became companionship, the "moral form of Eros."

Ideal and reality

Philosophies and ideals are all very well. In older times they did not admit of differences in gender, class, or age. Intellectual systems of ideas were constructed either as abstractions that rose *above* society, or that were *part of* society, as defined by the men of the elite. We must search much nearer to our own time, and in other sources, if we are to find evidence for the idea that friendship is anything more than a relationship between men, whether our search takes us to autobiographies, correspondence, or learned treatises. Yet surely in all periods women were just as incapable as men of living without the friendship of others. I have taken a handful of examples of how individuals formed friendships in the seventeenth and eighteenth centuries. This material does not reveal any unequivocal differences between men and women's ways of looking at friendship. A certain tendency to prefer the company of other gentlemen can be seen in Turner the merchant, and of ladies in Catharina Wallenstedt, but neither circle was completely unisexual. Variations in the choice of friendship can probably be explained by the gender patterns characteristic of the period. In the older period men moved in wider social circles, and found friends through their work or profession. Women adopted their husband's friends, but also made their own in their immediate circle. But there is nothing to indicate that men and women defined friendship or viewed their friends differently.

Friendship, however, was not always seen as an ideal that merited realization. An issue well worth raising is why, in certain circumstances, friendship was rather viewed as a threat, or at best as something questionable, in a particular culture or period. Certain specific situations and settings seem to lend themselves to such concerns, as I have shown. In the world of the Icelandic sagas, friendship was obviously considered as highly dangerous as it was beneficial and essential to survival. The paradox stemmed from the fact that friends entered into a pact that meant they had an obligation to help each other, no matter what. Embarking on a friendship could be risky in the extreme. Mediaeval monasticism in turn was in certain phases liable to view individual friendships as a threat to community solidarity, a threat to the brotherhood of the religious. Yet friendship, be it for personal profit or pleasure, was quite simply essential

195

in all walks of life, from the humblest village to the royal court. Favors were given and returned, gifts given and received, all under the auspices of friendships that operated in the grey area between private and public. In due course this would come to be seen as a problem, as I have shown with examples from Swedish history. As the very earliest mediaeval national law codes demonstrate, the Swedish authorities had long been aware that the legal process would be jeopardized if they could not prevent individuals giving false testimony on behalf of friends. In the sixteenth, seventeenth, and eighteenth centuries the central government became increasingly alert to the risks of friendship in official contexts. The government needed faithful public servants who followed the rules and whose loyalty was primarily to the State, and not to their close friends. For this reason, warnings of the risks of friendship were issued to people in positions of particular responsibility, not least amongst them judges and court witnesses.

Other forms of threatening friendship were those that the world viewed with suspicion because they seemed too intimate. There were sporadic warnings in the Middle Ages that homosexuality would result from close friendships between monks, and in the sixteenth and seventeenth centuries that sailors and soldiers were similarly susceptible. In like fashion, there was sometimes alarm in the nineteenth century at "passionate" friendships between women. It was a time when scientists were only too willing to analyze on women's sexuality, and the word lesbian first gained currency.[5]

Interestingly, the first legislative moves to prevent cronyism by regulating friendship coincided in Protestant Scandinavia with the attempt to control love and sexuality more strictly than before. I have been able to demonstrate how the post-Reformation Swedish State and Church worked together to safeguard love and sexuality between spouses. Within marriage men and women had a right to enjoy each other's bodies, as Luther saw it, and where a marriage was founded on true love, it was thought more likely to last. The debate amongst the Lutheran Church authorities had little to do with enforcing marriages of convenience or making the case for sexual continence; instead it centered on the fact that the sacrament of marriage should be based on love, that healthy marital sexuality was welcome, and that if possible more children should be born. It was only logical that the law should safeguard matrimony. As a result, following the Reformation—and in Sweden, above all, the Supplementary Law in 1608—a whole series of sexual behaviors were criminalized and could result in draconian punishments: incest, bestiality, male homosexuality, adultery, and fornication.

However, there is every indication that it was not only the Church and State that adhered to the value systems that underpinned this unusually effective control of sexuality, but also most of the agrarian population. There was a certain logic behind the maintenance of heterosexual norms and loving marriage, as most could see. In a sparsely populated agrarian society, one where most of the peasants owned their own land but rarely farmed on a large scale, manpower was needed if society was to survive. Children and women had to help the master of the house in his work. At the same time, it was important that the master and mistress of the household had legitimate children who could later inherit and take responsibility for future generations. Conversely, illegitimate children upset the scheme of things. They were a potential source of conflict, and the parish as a whole or the Church in particular ran the risk of paying for their maintenance unless fathers at the very least could be forced to accept responsibility for their children.

The State, the Lutheran Church, and most ordinary Swedes seem to have shared the same views on this point: it was why neighbors were prepared to witness in court against adulterers; it was why a court officer might pass a lighter sentence if a young man promised to marry the girl he had got pregnant; it was why the State and Church could praise a woman who had been "the pillar of her household," and could decide that two young people who loved each other should be allowed to "come together" rather than force them into separate marriages of convenience; it was why the courts were prepared to look almost benevolently on two women who had duped the Church by marrying—like Ulrika Eleonora and Maria—because their life together was proper, and there was little risk of them producing children. In other words, there was not only a prescriptive discourse of forbidden sexuality in post-Reformation Sweden. There was also a positive discourse of love, and a broad recognition of the value of marriage in furthering not only the State's demographic interests, but also the local social order.

Today?

As we have seen, during the rise of modern society both friendship and sexuality were increasingly viewed as private concerns. Taking Sweden as an example, starting in the early nineteenth century most forms of heterosexuality between adults were decriminalized, and in the twentieth century homosexuality between adults followed suit. Friendship has been redefined as a private relationship that in principle has no bearing on public life, where it instead runs the risk of causing corruption.

But today, in our "late modern" society, there is a renewed interest in friendship networks, and friendship has attracted attention in the social sciences and the humanities in a very different way than was the case, say, at the start of the twentieth century. I would suggest the reason for this should be sought in the increased suspicion of modern institutions and a lack of faith in the ability of public bodies to solve people's problems. Social networks and personal relationships have been re-evaluated as necessary complements to the circumstances of real life, but also as scholarly problems.

This makes a global perspective all the more necessary. My discussions have dealt with European or Scandinavian discourses and—to some extent—also mentalities. Well may we wonder how exotic European notions of friendship appear in Africa or Asia, for example. A couple of years ago I attended a world congress on history in Sydney where I took part in an international panel to discuss informal relationships throughout history. An Indian economic historian and a Japanese historian were there, along with British, Australian, and Nordic historians. Initially our conversation turned on the similarities between our conclusions. Everyone was familiar with Aristotle's philosophy of friendship; everyone took for granted the existence of reciprocity and trust in informal relationships. We aired our general agreement on how friendship worked in terms of momentous social transformations such as religious movements, colonization, industrialization, or migration.

But gradually it became increasingly clear to me that my Indian colleague's premise was that friendship, like kinship, could be an inherited or even imposed relationship. Because of loyalties to clan, caste, or village, the tradition she studied did not have the same scope for the individual choice of close relationships as was the case in the West, she argued. A young boy in a little village in India would to a certain degree "inherit" all his parents' friends. Conversely, perhaps this means that people in other parts of the world are hit even harder when friendship—like kinship—is terminated by crucial historical processes such as, for example, the brutal traffic in slaves and economic migration. Whereas the Western tradition often has underscored friendship as a *voluntary relationship that creates integration and security*, the global perspective opened my eyes to the significance of *collectively communicable friendships* and of *involuntary rifts in personal relationships*. The exchange of ideas on the panel led us European participants to reflect self-critically on the Western self-image of individual choice. After all, we also have friends whom everyone in our families, regardless of generation, accepts and appreciates. And if it comes to that, we have also "inherited" some of our relationships. On the panel we recognized that a new field in international comparative studies was opening at our feet: not only friendships in varying social and cultural contexts across continents, but also—in the context of voluntary or forced migrations—broken friendships and the need for new close relationships.

Finally, what reach does the power of friendship have today beyond the individual's existential and moral space? Can it do more than aid personal development, or be a metaphor for the good things in life? Will it be possible in future to bridge the gap between circles of friends and the social structure in which they live, between private and public, as our ancestors once did in the past? The classical doctrine saw ideal friendship as a means to engage in the public sphere, a principle for social and political life. In modern times we are more used to seeing friendship as something private, as an end in itself. Friends who help each other in the public sphere are viewed with unease or suspicion. Network has a more comforting ring to it than boss rule or semi-secret society, but can in the worst cases display worrying similarities. Modernization has created a healthy scepticism about friendship's place in politics and the law.

But does this reservation mean that friendship has completely lost its political relevance? In my view this does not have to be the case. In my analysis of the seventeenth-century discourse, I referred to historians who have interpreted the egalitarian impulse in friendship as a visionary principle in a hierarchical culture. The centrality of reciprocity and equality to friendship might at best promote a process of peaceful cooperation. Ray Pahl believes there is a strong idealistic element to close friendship because it prises us from the ruts we are trapped in by status, role, or habit. Aristotle in his turn stands for the idea of a profound, communicative friendship in the name of virtue and wisdom. It could quite possibly offer a vision of society that transcends party politics—and for that reason alone is potentially dangerous to authority.[6] Trust as a necessary dimension of society is also attracting great interest amongst modern researchers; that same trust has always been integral to the definition of love and friendship.

In my opinion, in this situation there is a need for a renewed critical examination of historical examples of informal relationships. A debate on the complicated and ambiguous combinations of private and public networks in the early modern period—or even the profound reflection on human nature and the ideals of friendship in classical and mediaeval thinking—may prove useful to us in future.

Perhaps we might once again be inspired by the classical philosophy of friendship, interpreted as an ethical and political vision, and adapted to modern public life. This would mean following up, for example, Martha Nussbaum's discussion of Aristotle, or Jacques Derrida's book *The Politics of Friendship*.[7] Friendship in classical antiquity was a vision built on trust, reciprocity, and equality, but in Athens and Rome it was only ever applied to important men. To be relevant now, it would have to be extended to groups who were excluded from social decisions in the classical period: women, slaves, the dispossessed, and the disenfranchised. Inspired by such a vision, would it be possible to construct social systems and international relationships not as if we were enemies to be suspected and controlled, but as if we were friends, capable of trusting each other?

Notes

[1] Allan Silver, *Public and Private in Thought and Practice*, Chicago, 1998.

[2] For further discussion of the same themes, see Eva Österberg & Christina Carlsson Wetterberg, *Rummet vidgas. Kvinnor på väg ut i offentligheten ca 1880–1940*, Stockholm, 2002; for the discourses of the day, see Inger Hammar, *Emancipation och religion. Den svenska kvinnorörelsens pionjärer i debatt om kvinnans kallelse ca 1860–1900*, Stockholm, 1999; for women who used their networks for political ends in the struggle for suffrage, see Christina Florin, *Kvinnor får röst. Kön, känslor och politisk kultur i kvinnornas rösträttsrörelse*, Stockholm, 2006.

[3] For the Western inheritance of such ideas see chapter 2.

[4] See, for example, Lilian Faderman, *Surpassing the Love of Men. Romantic Friendship and Love between Women from the Renaissance to the Present*, London, 1997; and the discussion of Faderman and Swedish examples in Eva Österberg, *Vänskap—en lång historia*, pp. 158–170.

[5] See the discussion and references in Eva Österberg, "Förbjuden kärlek och förtigandets strategi. När Ulrika Eleonora gifte sig med Maria," in Eva Österberg, ed., *Jämmerdal och fröjdesal*, p. 275 ff.

[6] Ray Pahl, *On Friendship*, Polity, Oxford, 2000 p. 160 ff.

[7] Martha Nussbaum, *Love's Knowledge: Essays on Philosophy and Literature*, Oxford, New York 1992; Jacques Derrida, *Politics of Friendship*, London, 1997.

205

References

Alberoni, Francesco. *L'amicizia*. Milan: Garzanti Editore, 1984. (Swedish translation: *Vänskap*, Göteborg: Korpen 1987)

—. *Jag älskar dig*. Göteborg: Korpen, 1996.

Althoff, Gerd. *Verwandte, Freunde und Getreue. Zum politischen Stellenweer der Gruppenbindungen im früheren Mittelalter.* Darmstadt, 1990.

—. "Friendship and Political Order." In *Friendship in Medieval Europe*, ed. Julian Haseldine. Stroud, Gloucestershire: Sutton, 1999, pp. 91–105.

—. *Family, Friends and Followers: the Political Importance of Group Bonds in the Early Middle Ages.* New York. 2004.

Ambjörnsson, Ronny. "En kärlekshistoria." In *Divan 2006: 1-2.* Umeå: Umeå University Press, 2006.

Andersson, Irene. *Kvinnor mot krig. Aktioner och nätverk för fred 1914–1940.* Lund: Studia Historica Lundensis, 2001.

Ankarloo, Bengt. *Trolldomsprocesserna i Sverige.* Lund: Rättshistoriskt bibliotek, 1971.

Ankarloo, Bengt & Henningsen, Gustav, eds. *Häxornas Europa 1400–1700.* Lund: Rättshistoriska studier, 1987.

Ankarloo, Bengt. "Om historiens nytta." In *Ut med historien*, eds. Lars Edgren & Eva Österberg. Lund: Lund University Press, 1992.

Aristotle. *The Nichomachean Ethics.* Translated by J. E. C. Welldon. New York: Prometheus Books, 1987.

Aronsson, Peter. *Bönder gör politik. Det lokala självstyret som social arena i tre smålandssocknar.* Lund: Lund University Press, 1992.

Augustine, of Hippo. *De civitate Dei* XIX (3), trans. Henry Bettenson. Harmondsworth, 1984.

—. *Confessions.* Trans. Henry Chadwick. Oxford: Harvard University Press, 1991.

Bauman, Zygmunt. *Intimations of Post-Modernity.* New York, 1992.

Behre, Göran & Lars-Olof Larsson & Eva Österberg. *Sveriges historia 1521–1809. Stormaktsdröm och småstatsrealitet.* Stockholm: Liber, 2001.

Bergenlöv, Eva. *Skuld och oskuld. Barnamord och barnkvävning i rättslig diskurs och praxis omkring 1680–1800.* Lund: Lund University Press, 2004.

Bergner, Barbro. "Dygden som levnadskonst. Kvinnliga dygdeideal under stormaktstiden." In *Jämmerdal och fröjdesal. Kvinnor i stormaktstidens Sverige,* ed. Eva Österberg. Stockholm: Atlantis, 1997.

Birgitta, Den heliga (St). *Himmelska uppenbarelser IV,* trans. Tryggve Lundén. Malmö, 1958.

Bokholm, Sif. *En kvinnoröst i manssamhället. Agda Montelius 1850–1920.* Stockholm: Stockholmia, 2000.

Braddick, Michael J. *The Nerves of State. Taxation and the financing of the English State, 1558–1714.* Manchester and New York, 1996.

—. *State Formation in Early Modern Europe, c 1550–1700.* Cambridge: Cambridge University Press, 2000.

Brown, Peter. *Augustine of Hippo. A Biography*. Los Angeles, 1967.

Byock, Jesse. *Feud in the Icelandic Saga*. Berkeley and Los Angeles: University of California Press, 1988.

Cavarero, Adriana. *Relating Narratives. Storytelling and Selfhood*. London, 2000.

Cicero. *De senectute, de amicitia, de divinatione*. Trans. by W. A. Falconer. Cambridge, Mass and London: Harvard University Press, 1979.

Clover, Carol & Lindow, John. *Old Norse-Icelandic Literature. A Critical Guide*. Ithaca, 1981.

Collstedt, Christopher. *Duellanten och rättvisan*. Lund: Sekel, 2007.

Dahl, Gunnar. *Trade, Trust and Networks. Commercial Culture in Late Medieval Italy*. Lund: Nordic Academic Press, 1988.

Darnton, Robert, *The Literary Underground of the Old Regime*. Cambridge, Mass.: Harvard University Press, 1982.

Davis, Natalie Zemon & Arlette Farge. *A History of Women: Renaissance and Enlightenment Paradoxes*. Cambridge, Mass: Harvard University Press, 1993.

Davis, Natalie Zemon. *The Gift in Sixteenth-century France*. Oxford, 2000.

Dekker, Rudolf & Lotte van de Pol. *Vrouwen in mannenkleren*. Amsterdam, 1989.

Derrida, Jacques. *Politics of Friendship*. London: Verso, 1997.

Duby, Georges. "Introduction." In *A History of Private Life II. Revelations of the Medieval World*, eds. Philippe Ariès and Georges Duby. Cambridge, Mass. and London: Harvard University Press, 1988.

Dürrenberger, E. Paul & Gísli Pálsson. " The Importance of Friendship in the Absence of States, according to the Icelandic Sagas." In *The Anthropology of Friendship. Beyond the Community of Kinship*, eds. S. Bell & S. Coleman. Oxford: Berg, 1999.

Elmroth, Ingvar. *För kung och fosterland.* Lund: Lund University Press, 1981.

Fagerlund, Solveig. *Handel och Vandel. Vardagslivets sociala struktur ur ett kvinnoperspektiv. Helsingborg ca 1680– 1709.* Lund: Lunds University Press, 2002.

Fleck, Ludwik. *Uppkomsten och utvecklingen av ett vetenskapligt faktum.* Eslöv: Symposion, 1997.

Florin, Christina. *Kvinnor får röst. Kön, känslor och politisk kultur i kvinnornas rösträttsrörelse.* Stockholm: Atlas, 2006.

Foucault, Michel. *Histoire de la sexualité I: La volonté de savoir.* Paris: Gallimard, 1976.

—. *Histoire de la sexualité I-III.* Paris: Gallimard, 1976– 1984.

—. *The Hermeneutics of the Subject: lectures at the Collège de France.* New York, 2004.

Giddens, Anthony. *The Nation-state and Violence.* Cambridge: Polity, 1985.

—. *The Consequences of Modernity.* Cambridge: Polity, 1990.

—. *Modernity and Self-Identity. Self and Society in the Late Modern Age.* Cambridge: Polity, 1991.

Gisle Surssons Saga, ed. Hjalmar Alving. Stockholm, 1979.

Grette Asmundssons Saga, ed. Hjalmar Alving. Stockholm, 1979.

Gurevich, Aron. *Medieval popular culture. Problems of belief and perception.* Cambridge and Paris: Cambridge University Press, 1988.

—. *The Origins of European Individualism.* Oxford: Oxford University Press, 1995. (Swedish translation: *Den svårfångade individen.* Stockholm: Ordfront, 1997.)

Guttormsson, Loftur. "The Development of Popular Religious Literacy in the Seventeenth and Eighteenth Century." In *Scandinavian Journal of History* 1990:1, Stockholm.

Habermas, Jürgen. *The Structural Transformation of the Public Sphere. An Inquiry into a Category of Bourgeois Society.* Trans. T. Burger with the assistance of F. Lawrence. Cambridge: University Press, 1962, 1989.

Hammar, Inger. *Emancipation och religion. Den svenska kvinnorörelsens pionjärer i debatt om kvinnans kallelse ca 1860-1900.* Stockholm. Carlssons, 1999.

Hardwick, Julie. *The Practice of Patriarchy. Gender and Politics of Household in Early Modern France.* Pennsylvania University Press, 1998.

Hay, Douglas. "Property, Authority, and the Criminal

Law." In *Albion's Fatal Tree. Crime and Society in Eighteenth-Century England*, eds. D. Hay, P. Linebaugh & E.P. Thompson, London: Allen Lane, 1975.

Haystrup, Helge. *Augustinstudier 12: Naestekaerlighedens problematik*. Copenhagen, 2000.

Helgason, Jón. *Hjärtats skrifter. En brevkulturs uttryck i korrespondensen mellan Anna Louisa Karsch och Johann Wilhelm Ludwig Gleim*. Lund: Lund University Press, 2007.

Hermanson, Lars. *Släkt, vänner och makt. En studie av elitens politiska kultur i 1100-talets Danmark*. Göteborg: Gothenburg University Press, 2000.

—. *Bärande band. Vänskap, kärlek och brödraskap i det medeltida Nordeuropa, ca 1000–1200*. Lund: Nordic Academic Press, 2009.

Hermanson, L., T. Småberg, & J. Danneskiold-Samsöe, eds. *Vänner, patroner och klienter. Norden 900-1800*. Report to the 26th Nordic history conference, Reykjavik 8–12 August 2007. Reykjavik, 2007.

Hunt, Lynn. *Measuring Time, Making History*. The Natalie Zemon Davis Lectures. Budapest – New York: Central European University Press, 2008.

Kierkegaard, Sören. *Antingen – eller, ett livsfragment, 1–2*. Önneköp: Nimrod, 2002.

Koselleck, Reinhart. "Einleitung." In *Geschichtliche Grundbegriffe. Historisches Lexikon zur politisch-sozialen Sprache in Deutschland, Bd 1*, eds. Otto Brunner, Werner Conze & Reinhart Kosselleck. Stuttgart, 1972.

212

—. *Vergangene Zukunft. Zur Semantik geschichtliche Zeiten.* Frankfurt am Main: Suhrkampf, 1979.

Larsson, Lars-Olof. *På marsch mot evigheten. Svensk stormaktstid i släkten Stålhammars spegel.* Stockholm: Prisma, 2007.

Lennartsson, Malin. *I Säng och Säte.* Lund: Lund University Press, 1999.

Lerner, Gerda. *The Creation of Feminist Consciousness from the Middle Ages to Eighteen-seventy.* Oxford: Oxford University Press, 1994.

Lilieqvist, Jonas. "Peasants against Nature. Crossing the Boundaries between Man and Animal in Seventeenth and Eighteenth Century Sweden." In *Journal of the History of Sexuality,* vol. 1:3, 1991.

—. *Brott, synd och straff. Tidelagsbrottet i Sverige under 1600- och 1700-talen.* Umeå, 1992.

—. "Staten och sodomiten – tystnaden kring homosexuella handlingar i 1600- och 1700-talens Sverige." In *Lambda nordica vol 1.* Stockholm, 1995.

Lindberg, Bo H. *Praemia et poenae. Etik och straffrätt i Sverige i tidig ny tid.* Manuscript, 1992.

Lindstedt Cronberg, Marie. *Synd och Skam. Ogifta mödrar på svensk landsbygd 1680–1880.* Lund: Lund University Press, 1997.

Lindstedt Cronberg, Marie & Catharina Stenqvist. *Förmoderna livshållningar. Dygder, värden och kunskapsvägar från antiken till upplysningen.* Lund, 2008.

Lorin, Claude. *Pour Saint Augustin*. Paris, 1988.

Lönnroth, Lars. *Skaldemjödet i berget. Essayer om fornisländsk ordkonst och dess återanvändning i nutiden.* Stockholm: Atlantis, 1996.

Luhman, Niklas. *Trust and Power.* New York, 1979.

Lundgren, Britta. *Den ofullkomliga vänskapen.* Stockholm, 1995.

Magnúsdóttir, Audur. "Kärlekens makt eller maktens kärlek. Om frilloväsende och politik hos Oddaverjarna." Conference paper, 1999.

Macfarlane, Alan. *The Family Life of Ralph Josselin. A Seventeenth-Century Clergyman. An Essay in Historical Anthropology.* Cambridge: Cambridge University Press, 1970.

Mann, Michael. "The Autonomous Power of the State: its Origins, Mechanisms and Results." In *States in History*, ed. John A. Hall. Oxford: Oxford University Press, 1986.

McGuire, Brian. *Friendship and Community. The Monastic Experience 350–1250.* Kalamanzoo: Cistercian Publications, 1988.

McNamara, Marie Aquinas. *Friendship in Saint Augustine.* Friburg, 1958.

Melberg, Arne. *Försök att läsa Montaigne.* Stehag: Symposion, 2000.

Miller, William Ian. *Feud, Law and Society in Saga Iceland.* Ithaca and London, 1990.

—. *Humiliation. And Other Essays on Honor, Social Discomfort, and Violence.* Ithaca and London, 1993.

Misztal, Barbara. *Trust in Modern Societies. The Search for the Bases of Social Order.* Cambridge, 1996.

Misch, Georg. *Geschichte der Autobiographie.* Bern und Frankfurt, 1949–62.

Montaigne, Michel de. *Essays,* trans. John Florio & Charles Cotton. London, 1800. (Swedish translation: *Essayer, Bok I-II.* Stockholm: Atlantis, 1986)

Monter, William. "Protestant Wives, Catholic Saints, and the Devil's Handmaid: Women in the Age of Renaissance." In *Becoming Visible. Women in European History,* eds. Renate Bridenthal, Claudia Coontz & Susan Stuard. Boston: Harvard University Press, 1987.

Naess, Hans-Eyvind & Eva Österberg. "Sanctions, Agreement, Sufferings." In *People Meet the Law. Control and Conflict-Handling in the Courts,* eds. Eva Österberg, & Sölvi Bauge Sogner. Oslo: Universitetsforlaget, 2000.

Nussbaum, Martha. *Love's Knowledge. Essays on Philosophy and Literature.* Oxford and London, 1992.

Njals Saga. Trans. Magnús Magnusson & Hermann Pálsson. London, 1960.

Österberg, Eva. *Kolonisation och kriser.* Lund: Liber, 1977.

Österberg, Eva & Dag Lindström. *Crime and Social Control in Medieval and Early Modern Swedish Towns.* Uppsala: Aömqvist & Wiksell Intenational, 1988.

Österberg, Eva. *Mentalities and Other Realities.* Lund: Lund University Press, 1991.

—. "Social Arena or Theatre of Power? The Courts,

Crime, and the Early Modern State in Sweden." In *The-atres of Power. Social Control and Criminality in Historical Perspective*, ed. Heikki Pihlajamäki. Jyväskylä: Publications of Matthias Calonius Society I., 1991.

—. *Folk förr. Historiska essäer.* Stockholm: Atlantis, 1995.

—, ed. *Jämmerdal och fröjdesal. Kvinnor i stormaktstidens Sverige.* Stockholm: Atlantis, 1997.

—. "Förbjuden kärlek och förtigandets strategi. När Ulrika Eleonora gifte sig med Maria." In *Jämmerdal och fröjdesal. Kvinnor i stormaktstidens Sverige*, ed. Eva Österberg. Stockholm: Atlantis, 1997.

—. "På samhällsstegens högsta topp. Drottning eller husfru." In *Jämmerdal och fröjdesal. Kvinnor i stormaktstidens Sverige*, ed. Eva Österberg. Stockholm: Atlantis, 1997.

—. "State Formation and the People. The Swedish Model in Perspective." In *Gemeinde, reformation und Wideerstand*, eds. H. R. Schmidt, André Holenstein & Andreas Würgler. Tübingen, 1998.

Österberg, Eva & Sölvi Bauge Sogner, eds. *People Meet the Law. Control and Conflict-handling in the Courts.* Oslo: Universitetsforlaget, 2000.

Österberg, Eva & Erling Sandmo. "Introduction." In *People Meet the Law. Control and Conflict-handling in the Courts*, eds. Eva Österberg & Sölvi Bauge Sogner. Oslo: Universitetsforlaget, 2000.

Österberg, Eva & Christina Carlsson Wetterberg. *Rummet*

vidgas. Kvinnor på väg ut i offentligheten ca 1880-1940.
Stockholm: Atlantis, 2002.

Österberg, Eva. "Vänskap—hot eller skydd i medeltidens samhälle. En existentiell och etisk historia." In *Historisk Tidskrift 2003:4*, pp. 549 –572. Stockholm: Historiska föreningen, 2003.

—. "Våldets känslorum. Berättelser om makt och moral i det förmoderna samhället." In *Våldets mening. Makt, minne, myt*, eds. Eva Österberg & Marie Lindstedt Cronberg. Lund: Nordic Academic Press, 2004.

Österberg, Eva & Marie Lindstedt Cronberg, eds. *Kvinnor och våld. En mångtydig kulturhistoria.* Lund: Nordic Academic Press, 2005.

Österberg, Eva. "Krigens moral och fredens lycka. Kvinnor om våldet på 1600-talet." In *Kvinnor och våld. En mångtydig kulturhistoria*, eds. Eva Österberg & Marie Lindstedt Cronberg. Lund: Nordic Academic Press, 2005.

—. *Vänskap—en lång historia.* Stockholm: Atlantis, 2007.

—. "Vännerna och jaget. Att bli individ tillsamans med andra." In *Förmoderna livshållningar. Dygder, värden och kunskapsvägar från antiken till upplysningen*, eds. Marie Lindstedt Cronberg & Catharina Stenqvist. Lund: Nordic Academic Press, 2008.

Östlund, Joachim. *Lyckolandet. Maktens legitimering i officiell retorik från stormaktstid till demokratins genombrott.* Lund: Sekel, 2007.

Pahl, Ray. *On Friendship*. Cambridge: Polity, 2000.

Petrarch. *My secret book*. Trans. John Gordon Nichols. Hesperus, 2002.

Persson, Fabian. *Servants of Fortune. The Swedish Courts between 1598 and 1721*. Lund: Lund University Press, 1999.

Petri, Olaus. *Några allmänna regler där en domare skall sig alldeles efter rätta*. Stockholm, 1960.

Reuterswärd, Elisabeth. *Ett massmedium för folket. Studier i de allmänna kungörelsernas funktion i 1700-talets samhälle*. Lund: Lund University Press, 2001.

Revera, Margareta. "En barock historia." In *Tre Karlar: Karl X Gustav, Karl XI, Karl XII*, ed. Gudrun Ekstrand. Stockholm: Nationalmuseum, 1984.

Ricoeur, Paul. *Time and Narrative*. Chicago, 1984.

—. *Oneself as Another*. Chicago and London, 1992.

Roper, Lyndal. *The Holy Household. Women and Morals in Reformation Augsburg*. Oxford and New York: Oxford University Press, 1991.

Rousseau, Jean-Jacques. *Confessions*, trans. Angela Scholar. Oxford, 2000.

Schmitt, Jean-Claude. "La découverte de l'individu: une fiction historiographique." In *La fabrique, la figure et la feinte: Fictions et statut des fictions en psychologie*, eds. P. Mengal, & F. Parot. Paris, 1989.

Shannon, Laurie. *Sovereign Amity. Figures of Friendship in Shakespearean Contexts*. Chicago and London: University of Chicago Press, 2002.

Sigurdsson, Jón Vidar. "Friendship in the Icelandic Commonwealth." In *From Sagas to Society. Comparative Approaches to Early Iceland*, ed. Gísli Pálsson. Reykjavik: Hisarlik Press, 1992.

Silver, Allan. *Public and Private in Thought and Practice*. Chicago, 1988.

Småberg, Maria. *Ambivalent Friendship. Anglican Conflicthandling and Education for Peace in Jerusalem 1920–1948*. Lund: Lund University Press, 2005.

Sogner, Sölvi, Marie Lindstedt Cronberg & Hilde Sandvik. "Women in Court." In *People Meet the Law. Control and Conflict-handling in the Courts*, eds. Eva Österberg & Sölvi Bauge Sogner. Oslo Universitetsforlaget, 2000.

Svare, Helge. *Vennskap*. Oslo: Pax Forlag, 2004.

Tadmor, Naomi. *Family and Friends in Eighteenth-Century England. Household, Kinship, and Patronage*. Cambridge: Cambridge University Press, 2001.

—. "Revisiting the public sphere and the history of the family" in *Vänskap över gränser. En festskrift till Eva Österberg*, eds. Kenneth Johansson & Marie Lindstedt Cronberg. Lund, 2007.

Tilly, Charles. *Coercion, Capital and European States, AD 990–1990*. Oxford: Oxford University Press, 1990.

Thunander, Rudolf. *Hovrätt i funktion. Göta hovrätt och brottsmålen 1635–1699*. Stockholm: Rättshistoriskt bibliotek, 1993.

Vico, Giambattista. *Självbiografi*. Stockholm: Atlantis, 1999.

Wiesner, Merry E. "Spinning out capital. Women's work in early Modern Economy." In *Becoming visible. Women in European History*, eds. Renate Bridenthal, Claudia Coontz & Susan Stuard. Boston: Harvard University Press, 1987.

Wolff, Charlotta. *Vänskap och makt. Den svenska politiska eliten och upplysningstidens Frankrike*. Jyväskylä: Svenska litteratursällskapet i Finland, 2005.

Index[1]

---

[1] It should be noticed that the index does not include names of authors in footnotes unless they are also explicitly referred to in the main text of the book.

225